THE
ENCYCLOPEDIA
OF HARDWARE

THE ENCYCLOPEDIA OF HARDWARE

TOM PHILBIN

HAWTHORN BOOKS, INC.
Publishers/NEW YORK
A Howard & Wyndham Company

CONTENTS

I

General Hardware

II

Miniature Hardware

III

Electrical Hardware

IV

Plumbing Hardware

Acknowledgments

No book is the product—an appropriate word!—of one person. That is emphatically true in this case. The quality of the information is only as good as the people it comes from. In this case, I was fortunate.

Specifically, my thanks to Len Micene, Pete Ray of Four Shores Electrical Supply for information on electrical products, to Gil Carll, and to Chuck Kowalsky of J. P. Krevtzer, Inc., for information on plumbing, and to Warren Deming and Fritz Koelbel for information on everything else. My profound thanks to all. And finally, thanks to Terri Micene, my typist, who endured much, and to my wife, Catherine, who thinks the book is great. Then again, a friend once told her that she'd think my shopping list was great.

Introduction

This book is designed to help the do-it-yourselfer in a number of ways.

First, it presents a comprehensive overview of the kinds of general hardware, electrical hardware, and plumbing hardware that are available in most retail stores. You may well be able to solve a problem just by knowing that a certain product exists.

Second, while not essentially a buying guide, the book does make sharp distinctions among various products. It explains not only how similar products differ from each other but recommends the one preferred for a specific job. For example, a flat washer should be used for new plumbing work, a beveled washer for a repair job.

Third, there are tips on product use. Although the book makes no attempt to compete with in-depth how-to manuals, there are instances where special tips or specific step-by-step instructions are called for. For example, not many people realize how easy—and inexpensive—it is to replace old screening. Since directions are rarely supplied when the products are purchased, complete instructions are given here. Today, however, most hardware products come "carded," with the product on the front and installation instructions on the reverse side. These readily available instructions have not been repeated in the book.

Fourth, the do-it-yourselfer should be able to locate without difficulty the products discussed here. Only those products commonly available have been included. So whether you live in a city or in a rural community, you should be able to walk up to the counter of your supplier, ask for a product, and get it. In the few cases where specialized products could be difficult to locate, mail-order sources are specified.

The first step in locating any product is, of course, to ask at the store. And—most emphatically—to bring the old product to show. If your dealer doesn't have a product, he may be able to get it from his local supplier. If all else fails, return to the book, check the appendix for the address of the manufacturer, and write directly.

There are many different places to shop for hardware. You can purchase an electrical switch at a general hardware store, an electrical supply store, a five and dime, a discount home center—any number of places. For the best selection, however, I would recommend the following: For general hardware go to a well-stocked hardware store. For plumbing fixtures go to a plumbing supply store that services the retail trade, and for electrical products a retail electrical supply store. Not only will you find a larger selection at a specialty store but you will also find countermen who know their products and can supply custom-tailored advice. By all means utilize it.

Finally, the telephone can save you some time and effort. Before you go to a store that you're not pretty sure has a product you're looking for, give them a ring. The Yellow Pages can be helpful in locating likely stores to begin with.

Tips on Using This Book

In order to use this book to the best possible advantage, it is suggested that you familiarize yourself—at least in a passing way—with the entire contents. Perhaps the quickest way to do this is to pore over the photos and drawings, since the vast majority of products discussed in the text are illustrated.

Familiarizing yourself with the contents can reward you in several ways. First, it will alert you to the existence of a product you may not have known about. For example, if you were doing a framing job, you might automatically turn to the sections on nails or screws. But in some instances framing fasteners might be a better choice. There is an entire section on the subject.

Second, the book may enable you to combine products for a desired result when no single product seems to solve a problem. For example, I recently had some flakeboard plaques to hang. The only problem was that there were no hangers on the backs. I was aware, though, of wood screws and wire and picture hangers. It was a simple matter to drive a couple of small wood screws into the plaques, string wire between them, then suspend the plaques from the picture hooks I mounted in the wall.

Finally, knowledge of products can have a serendipitous result. For example, I recently needed a few things from a hardware store and I also needed some chain for a flush valve ball in a toilet tank. Knowing that hardware stores sell narrow brass chain, I was able to get a piece cut to the size I needed and saved a trip to the plumbing supply store.

In essence, start by getting an overview of the contents of the book. It is your personal hardware store, and you should know what is in it.

Confusion can reign when it comes to picking hardware according to the metal or finish used in making it. Following then, is some information that should clear things up.

Brass versus brass plated. Many hardware items are made of pure brass. Brass is a fairly soft metal, but it is weatherproof. It may be used inside or outside the house. It has to be used with care around salt water, however, because this can make it corrode.

Brass plated is simply steel that has been coated with brass. It is not weather proof.

Bronze. This is also available in pure form, and as such is weatherproof. Items made of it can be used inside or outside the house. It does not corrode; indeed, it is often used in marine applications. Bronze is also a very strong metal.

Bronze Plated. Like brass plated, this is steel that is coated with bronze. Unlike pure bronze, however, it will not stand up to weather.

Galvanized. This is a special kind of finish applied to steel items. The galvanizing may be hot-dipped or coated—technically, electroplated. The hot dipped galvanizing is far the superior of the two. Both are weatherproof. Most outdoor items are galvanized.

Zinc or cadmium plated. These terms are really synonymous. It is a wash coating that is given to hardware that makes them rust resistant but not rustproof. Galvanized items are far superior to ones with zinc or cadmium finishes.

Blued. This is hardly a finish but just a treatment given to items to keep them from rusting in the box while waiting to be sold.

Japanned. This is a baked enamel finish, but only about as weather resistant as items that are blued.

Chrome plated. This is a highly polished finish used on cabinet hardware and many plumbing items. It is highly resistant to corrosion and quite good-looking.

Many items come with no finish at all—just a plain steel. Other items, however, such as bolts, are "oiled" (given a black oillike coating). In no way should oiled items be considered weather resistant.

In selecting hardware items, pay careful attention to the finish and metal used. While some are better than others, it is the final application that should count, because it is a good way to save money. For example, you will pay about twice as much for a galvanized machine bolt than a plain one. It is good to use the right piece of hardware, but there can be too much of a good thing.

THE
ENCYCLOPEDIA
OF HARDWARE

GENERAL
HARDWARE

Cabinet Hardware

Hardware for cabinets can be grouped under three headings: hinges, catches, and knobs or pulls.

Hinges

Hinges are made for three kinds of doors: lipped, overlay, and flush. The lipped door is one in which a lip has been cut completely around the door. The overlay door is cut larger all around than the opening so that its edges rest on the cabinet frame. Flush doors ride inside the frame with their faces flush with the frame face. Each door style dictates the type of hinge that may be used on it.

There are various kinds of hinges, each designed to be used with one or more of these kinds of doors.

One of the most popular hinges is the pivot style. It is designed for use on the overlay door. One hinge is mounted on the top of the door and one on the bottom, with portions of each hinge bent over and screw mounted to frame and door. The result is a concealed hinge.

If you prefer a hinge that lets you automatically close the door, consider the self-closing type. This has a light spring inside that does this. This type of hinge can be used for any type of door—lip, overlay, or flush.

Butterfly hinges are so called because when fully opened they have the shape of a butterfly. They are for flush-door ap-

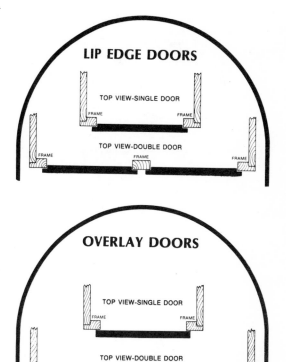

Flush door

Top view of flush door

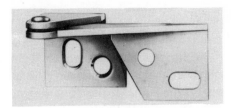

Pivot hinge

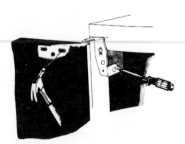

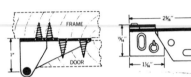

Top view of pivot hinge

Self-closing hinge

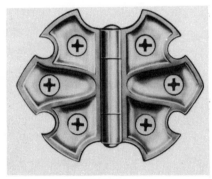

Pivot hinge installation

plication only. Many people also like them on cabinet lids. They can add an effective, decorative touch, particularly if they're made of brass, which many are.

Hinges vary greatly in size and thickness as well as style. The best way to ensure that you'll get the right pair is to take the existing pair to the hardware store with you. If you can match it up, it should be easy to install. Most manufacturers card hinges and provide complete installation instructions; some even turn the card into a tool: It becomes the template for making the screw holes. Most hinges have the manufacturer's name stamped on them. This should help you in locating the proper hinge.

For information on other types of hinges, see page 5.

Hinges come in a variety of finishes, but chrome is the most common. Antiqued copper, black, and brass (either plated or pure brass) are also quite common.

You'll likely want to match the hinge to the style of knobs or pulls, and there is a wide variety of styles to choose from. For example, Belwith International, Ltd., makes antique brass hinges and pulls as well as matching units in black antique and white gold, among others. Weiser offers polished metal knobs, pulls, and hinges as well as etched hardware and Early American styles. Amerock offers, among other things, antique copper and bronze. Robin Hardware offers Mediterranean-style hardware.

Butterfly hinge

Catches

There are three kinds of catches commonly used to secure cabinet doors: magnetic, roller, and spring or friction.

A magnetic catch has some definite advantages over the other two types. One is that if the door warps, the magnetic catch will still be strong enough to close it; no matter where the door part of the catch is, the magnet is almost bound to grip it, because most magnets are of the floating kind and are self-adjusting. In other words, only part of the magnet needs to contact the catch on the door.

On a normal-size door you only need one catch. On a big door, two are advisable, one on the bottom and one on the top. Also, if you have a cabinet door with many boards, a heavy-duty catch will be called for.

The roller catch consists of two rollers set close together; a part on the door interlocks with them.

One other type of catch available is the spring (friction) type, good for when you don't want any hardware to show on a door—say, when you're using hidden pivot hinges, for instance. This catch, made for lipped doors, is simple to operate: You push the door closed and push it again to open it.

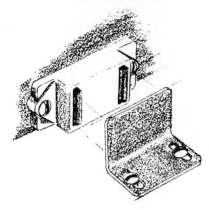

Magnetic catch

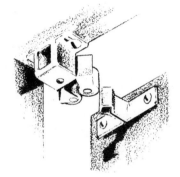

Roller catch

Knobs and Pulls

Knobs and pulls are simple to install. There are commonly one or two screws securing the hardware from the back side. You simply hold the knob or pull and turn the screws through predrilled holes in the door and into the knob or pull. In other cases, a screw is built into the knob, and you simply screw it to the door.

Besides the many styles made to coordinate with decorative hinges (see page 4), many companies also sell crystal (glass) and porcelain knobs and pulls. The variety is virtually endless, with much of the hardware beautifully crafted.

Knobs come in various styles to match other cabinet hardware.

Crystal (glass) knob

Pulls also come in various styles.

5

Casters

Casters come with a variety of features that should be married with the purpose you have in mind. In other words, get the casters that are right both for the job they're expected to do and for the place they're going to be used.

One thing to consider is the weight of the item. Putting casters on a heavy dresser is a far cry from installing them on a TV stand. Casters normally come boxed or carded, and the weight they can support will be noted. Indeed, the package commonly contains information on the kinds of things that particular set of casters is used for—beds, couches, refrigerators, and so on.

Consider also whether or not you want the casters to swivel 360°. This may be convenient on something like a dresser that you will want to roll out for cleaning, but very inconvenient on a refrigerator, which can slide all over the place if the casters swivel.

Do you want the casters to lock? There are locking types available that are especially handy on a bed that, if you happen to flop on it, may otherwise take you for a ride. Locking casters help ensure stability.

Caster wheels may be hard or soft, rubber or plastic. Each is designed to perform best on a specific kind of flooring. For example, hard rubber wheels would be used on concrete floors; soft rubber is good on resilient flooring (linoleum, inlay, and tile); plastic is good on carpet.

Casters also come with metal wheels. Most are strictly for heavy-duty use, but one worth singling out is the ball-type caster used on furniture—such as upholstered chairs—where looks count. These are available in a variety of fine finishes (brass, chrome) and add a decorative touch to the furniture. This caster is good for carpeted surfaces.

Finally, you should consider the condition and style of the leg that the caster is going to be installed on. Casters come in either stem or plate types. In the stem style there is a metal tube sticking up from the caster. This caster is designed to be installed in a socket in the leg. On the plate type, there is a flat plate that is attached with screws. Stem casters may be used on existing socket or on tubular metal legs; plate casters are used where legs are solid. If the leg end is chewed up or very narrow, use the stem-style caster.

Wheel Sizes

Casters are available with different wheel sizes. A 2″ caster is one whose wheels have a 2″ diameter. The rule is that the larger the wheel, the easier the caster will roll. Stem sizes also vary in diameter and thickness.

Casters come in stem *(top)* and plate *(bottom)* styles.

Wide-wheel casters are specifically designed for use on beds.

Metal ball-type casters are good looking and can be used on carpeting or resilient flooring.

Ball-Bearing Casters

Ball-bearing casters do not use wheels, but rather ball bearings in a housing. These are high-quality casters and are quite expensive (Acme is one good brand). They don't roll as well as wheel casters but have this advantage: When mounted, only about ½″ projects; in other words, only ½″ in height is added to the item, rather than the 2″ or so that the average caster will add. Consider them, then, where there is a shortage of headroom.

Ball-bearing caster. It's good when headroom is limited.

Glides

Glides for furniture come in various and sundry styles and finishes and may be nailed or screwed to furniture legs. They protect a floor from rub marks at the same time as they make an item easier to move.

Glides come in various styles.

INSTALLATION TIPS

Replacement Installations

1. Pry out the old casters with a screwdriver.
2. Replace the old sockets. To remove them, a simple idea that usually works is to drive a 10-penny nail, head end first, into the socket until it forces open, clears, and catches under the spring top. Then pull out the nail and socket with a claw hammer or pliers. One or two screwdrivers forced under the teeth of the track plates might help to free them.
3. Tap the new sockets into place. Use a block of wood to protect the track plate.
4. Insert the caster stem full length into the socket. Strike the bottom of the wheel with your hand to lock the stem in place.

If the socket holes are enlarged and will not contain new sockets, wrap them with a piece of paper or cellophane tape to make a snug fit.

New Caster Installations

1. If the original height of the furniture is to be maintained, saw off the legs to accommodate the height of the casters. Measure the caster from the bottom of the wheel to the base of the socket (see illustration).
2. Drill a hole the size of the socket (usually ⅜″ diameter) straight into the center of the leg, 1½″ deep.
3. Follow steps 3 and 4 for replacement installations.

Plate Caster Installations

Be sure that the surface is sufficiently larger than the plate to accommodate screws. Drill pilot holes and fasten the plate with screws. Use bolts if the attachment is to thin wood or metal.

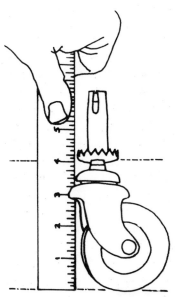

To keep the height of furniture the same on new caster installations, it is necessary to saw off the legs to a depth equal to the caster height (4″ in this case).

Tubular Metal Caster Installation

If for replacement, it is helpful to have a sample of the old caster for comparison purposes to determine proper socket size. If for a new installation, measure the tubing diameters, both inside diameter and outside diameter. To measure the inside diameter, use a triangular piece of cardboard. Insert the cardboard into the tubing mark, and measure as illustrated. Sockets are designated by outside diameter tubing dimension.

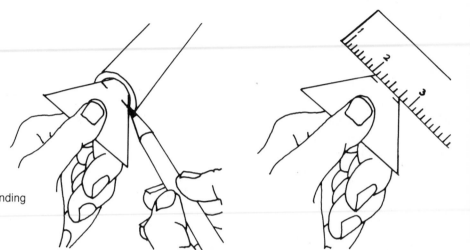

A wedge of cardboard is handy for finding the diameter on tubular metal legs.

Chain

Chain comes in perhaps thirty-five to forty different types, but the needs of most people will be amply filled by the chain available at hardware stores or other outlets. They commonly sell chain off 100′ reels, and you can get it cut to whatever length you wish.

Chain can be divided into two groups: chain for decorative use and chain whose primary function is strength. No matter what chain you get, however, you should observe what is known in the trade as the working-load limit. All chain is tested for this. It indicates the maximum amount of stress a chain can safely take under a steady pull.

Chain may not be thought of as a decorative material by many people, but it has a wide variety of uses.

Load limits vary greatly, depending on the metal the chain is made of and its diameter—the thickness of the "wire." One-quarter-inch decorative brass jack chain, for example, has a working load limit of 10 pounds. But grade 30 proof coil chain, in the same diameter, has a working load limit of 1,250 pounds. Before you buy a chain, then, you should make sure that it is strong enough for the job at hand. The dealer will have to be able to furnish you with these limits. Following are some common types of chain.

Jack chain

Jack chain comes in a variety of sizes (down to links about ¼″ in diameter) and can be used for decoration and support. It is often used for hanging flowerpots, children's toys, and the like. It is available brass plated, hot galvanized, in bright zinc, and solid brass.

SINGLE JACK CHAIN

DOUBLE JACK CHAIN

Jack chain types

Machine Chain

This is a short-link welded chain (meaning that individual links are welded together). You'll see machine chain as overhead door chains, on tailgates, and with agricultural implements. Any welded chain is the strongest you can get.

STRAIGHT LINK

TWIST LINK

Machine chain comes in a couple of styles.

Grade 30 Proof Coil Chain

If you want something stronger than machine chain, this is a good choice. Chain of this type has a working load limit of 1,250 pounds in the ¼″ size. The ⁵⁄₁₆″ chain has a load limit of 1,900 pounds. If you want chain that's even stronger, use high-test chain or grade 70. Grade 30 chain comes in plain steel, bright zinc, and galvanized finishes.

Sash Chain

This is used for hanging double-hung windows. It is flat and rides over pulleys easily. You can think of it as a good replacement material for sash cords on double-hung windows. However, if you live in a place where sea air is present, sash chain is inadvisable. Even bronze sash chain can rust out. Rope is a better choice.

Sash chain

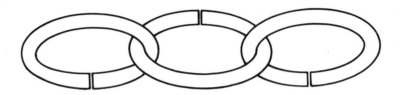

Safety, or plumber's, chain.

Safety, or Plumber's, Chain

This is another flat kind of chain commonly used by plumbers in toilet tanks. It is also a general utility chain and may be used for decorative purposes. It is available in bright zinc and solid brass.

Colored Decorative Chain

Decorative chain is available in colors and in links of various sizes and shapes. One company, ACCO (American Chain & Cable Company), makes such chain, which they call decor chain, in brass as well as in antique white, antique copper, and black finishes.

Decorative chain also comes in colors. You'll find it in the widest variety of colors when sold for plant hangers. Such light chain (and any light chain) can be pulled apart with pliers or fingers, an installation aid.

Packaged Chain

In addition to being available cut to length from reels, chain can be also be bought in packages or in assemblies prepared for particular uses. For example, American Chain and Cable has a bag with enough chain and fixtures for seven double-hung windows as well as a dog runner chain complete with swivel snaps at both ends (this chain is less likely to kink and twist

Chain for porch swings can be bought packaged, or you can make up your own. It should be mounted securely in the framing member with screw hooks.

How chain holds porch swing

than other types). Chain is also available in packages specifically intended for locking bikes, hanging porch swings, and for various vehicular jobs.

Bead Chain

Bead chain is made in quite a few sizes. In its catalogue the Bead Chain Company lists more than a dozen. In local stores, however, you'll usually only have a couple of sizes available. You can buy it by the foot from rolls, but it is also sold packaged, particularly as pulls for lamps. Bead chain may be hollow round beads (the balls are hollow and are joined by dumbbell-shaped connectors), or it may be a series of round and eliptically shaped beads. The major advantage of bead chain is that it will not kink. It can be twisted every which way and can then be shaken out straight again. It normally comes in chrome and brass finishes, with the latter, of course, more expensive. It is primarily used for decorative purposes around the home.

Dog runner chain. It comes with a swivel snap at one or both ends.

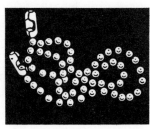

Bead chain comes individually wrapped, or you can buy it by the foot from reels. It is available in chrome or nickel plated.

USE TIP

Many of the lighter kinds of chain can be disconnected by prying apart links with your fingers. Or, use a pair of pliers. Pliers should be used to crimp the links shut.

Attachments and Accessories

A variety of accessories and attachments are available for chain. A common mistake, however, is to select an undersized attachment. It is important that the connector be sized to the chain; it must be just as strong as any link. Hardware dealers will have specific recommendations. Following are some of the more commonly used accessories.

S-hook. Like other attachments and accessories, it comes in various sizes. It should be crimped closed after being hooked onto the chain.

Left, clevis grab hook; *right,* clevis slip hook. They attach to the chain and in effect, make it work like a rope.

S-hook. This gets its name from the fact that it is shaped like the letter S. S-hooks come in various sizes and strengths and, as mentioned, should be equal to the strength of the chain they are attached to if the chain is under working load. Be aware, though, that S-hooks are *not* designed to be used for play equipment, backyard swings, or anything that requires a high standard of safety. S-hooks, after being attached, should be crimped with pliers so that the chain links can't slip out.

Clevis slip hook. This works like a lasso. The end of the hook is attached to one end of the chain; the hook is wide enough to slide along the chain but to grip when you want it to, so that in an application such as pulling out a tree stump, for example, you can get a tight hold before pulling the chain.

Clevis grab hook. This is shaped like a slip hook but is narrower. It can be hooked onto the outside of the chain between the links; hence, it's good for applications where you want a fixed loop in the chain.

Connecting links. Picture a chain link laid flat and cut in half and you have a connecting link. They are for permanently connecting lengths of chain and other attachments and do the same job as individual links. To form a connecting link, a rivet on one-half of the link is peened into an opening on the other half. Welding the parts makes the link even stronger, but it is not essential. To get the proper size connecting link, use the next larger size. For example, use a ⅜″ connecting link to join ⁵⁄₁₆″ chain.

Connecting link. It's like a fat letter C sliced in half horizontally.

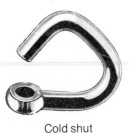

Cold shut

Swivel snaps. Swivel snaps snap onto whatever you wish and rotate 360° freely, allowing the chain to rotate freely also.

Cold shuts. These are also used to connect chain lengths or hooks. They are slipped onto a link (or hook) and hammered shut. Additional strength is gained by welding the point at which they connect.

Lap links. These are partially opened links that can be closed with a vise or hammer. They are for temporary joining and are not to be used where the safety of people or property would be endangered should they fail.

Rings. Welded rings are just that, rings available in a wide variety of sizes with many different uses.

Lap link. It is hammered or closed by vise action to join chain.

END OPEN

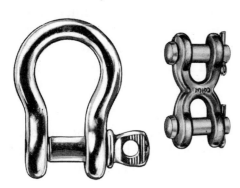

Other kinds of chain connectors

SAFETY TIPS
- Don't apply tension to a twisted chain.
- Don't overload a chain. Observe working-load limits.
- Don't jerk a chain from an at-rest condition; pull it gradually.
- Don't use a chain that looks deteriorated. Check for elongated links, a sign of imminent failure.

Closet Door Hardware

There are two kinds of special closet doors: sliding and bi-fold.

Sliding Doors

A sliding door consists of two panels, the track the door slides in and wheels that attach to the top of the door and ride in the track, which is fastened to the top of the door frame. Today very few, if any, manufacturers of sliding door hardware make track that mounts in the bottom of the closet opening.

Occasionally, when part of the door goes out of alignment or develops other problems, all that is needed is a simple adjustment. However, there are situations where a part fails to

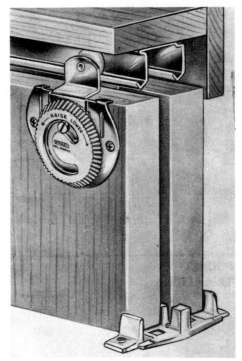

Sliding door hardware shown with door telescoped

13

Sheets and panels in various finishes and
styles are also available.

Sheet and Panels

This comes in solid and mesh form and in a variety of
finishes: plain, embossed, and gold anodized. One popular use
for the mesh is as a covering for cabinets; another is for
radiator covers. It is easily cut with snips.

Rods, Bars, and Angles

These can be cut with a hacksaw, are easily drilled, and can
be used for a number of different purposes, such as framework
for tables. Connections are made with sheet metal screws. Rod,
bar, and angles are available in lengths of 6' and 8' and in
varying thicknesses.

Solid aluminum comes in angle, bar, and
rod forms.

Tubing and Fittings

Tubing may be square or round. It ranges in size from an outside diameter of ¾″ to 1¼″ and comes in lengths of 6′ and 8′. The key to working with tubing is the range of fittings that is available. There is a variety of fittings that, like plumbing fittings, lets you join pieces of tubing at different angles. You can make 90°, T, and other connections. The fittings are shown in one of the photos. Tubing is cut with a hacksaw.

Key to being able to join aluminum tube are special connectors which are hammered in place.

Track is good for sliding doors and projects that involve sliding doors.

Track

Aluminum track for door panels and cabinet doors comes in various sizes in order to accommodate thick (plywood) or thin (plastic) materials.

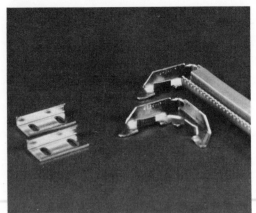

Connectors are used to join screen framing members (shown) and storm windows.

Framing members for do-it-yourself storm windows come with weatherstrip built on.

Storm and Screen Aluminum

Aluminum also comes in weather-stripped and plain frames for making screens and storm windows. The key here is the special corner locks that join frame members.

Reynolds publishes literature that shows how to use their products. These pamphlets should be available free at local stores. They also have a book that sells for $1.95 called *Repair, Improve, Create.*

Door Locks

There are two different kinds of locks for the home: exterior and interior.

In general, exterior locks are built more ruggedly than interior locks for reasons of security, and greater care is put into the design and finish.

Manufacturers make a tremendous variety of locks. Indeed, in preparing this book the author received product literature measuring 1½". However, there are types that are common and should serve you well in most situations.

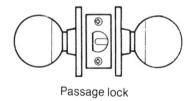

Passage lock

Privacy lock

Interior Locks

Interior locks are generally one of three kinds: passage, privacy, or bathroom.

Passage Lock. This type of lock has no locking mechanism. It can be opened from either side.

Privacy Lock. This type is generally used on bedrooms, where some degree of privacy is desired. These have a button inside which can be activated to close the door. Many come with a special key or rod enabling them to be opened from the outside. This is handy in case a child is locked in a room. A screwdriver can also be used to open the door.

Bathroom lock. A bathroom lock is exactly like a privacy lock, except that it is usually chrome plated to harmonize with other locks and hardware used in the bathroom. It also comes with a device to open it.

Closet locks. Some companies make closet locks. These are the same as passage locks except that the handles or knobs are smaller.

Exterior Locks.

Exterior cylinder lock sets usually operate in one of three different ways.

When the door is locked it can be opened and closed from the inside while the outside mechanism stays in the locked position. This type is often the villain when people lock themselves out.

Another type is one where the locked door can be opened from the inside but when you turn the knob it releases the locking mechanism and the door will remain unlocked from both sides. With this type you can't try the door to see if it is locked without unlocking it.

The third type is one where the door is locked and you cannot open it from the inside without first manually releasing a turn button. When that is released the door is unlocked on both sides.

All three of the locks just mentioned are available with different striking mechanisms. On some the bolt can be depressed even when the door is locked. This is a poor security lock. A burglar's trick is to use a plastic card to depress the bolt, opening the door. Other types of locks do not permit this, since the bolt will stay in the strike as long as a small rod adjacent to the strike remains depressed.

Exterior cylinder locks also come with keys for both the inside and outside of the door. These are sometimes used on glass doors. If the glass is broken by a burglar he won't be able to reach in and turn the handle to open the door without a key. Be aware, though, that in case you want to get out fast—say a fire starts—you'd better have the key nearby.

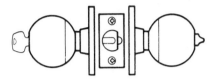

Exterior (entrance) lock

The bolt (latch) on this type of lock cannot be depressed by a burglar as long as the small rod adjacent to the bolt is depressed (it is in open position here).

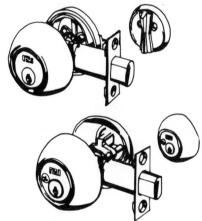

Two kinds of deadbolt locks. Lock at top may have the bolt turned by a key or lever inside. The bottom lock has two lock cylinders that work off the same key. It is especially designed for glass doors. If a burglar breaks through the glass panel, he can't open the door without a key. Be aware, though, that in case of fire this type of lock can be hazardous if you don't have key nearby.

Deadlocks

Commonly called deadbolt locks, these are generally the best locks for home security. They are of heavier construction than regular locks, and have no handle on the outside. Normally, there is a turn knob inside. When the bolt enters the strike it cannot be released without either turning it out with a key from the outside or, if keyless, turning the knob inside: The bolt does not have a spring action enabling someone to push it out of the strike. If the door is made of glass, you can get dead bolts with double cylinders—a key is needed for both the inside and outside cylinders: Like regular locks, the burglar would need a key for the inside cylinder.

Another type of deadbolt cannot be opened with a key from the outside as long as a button inside is activated.

Bolts on deadlocks come with varying "throws," the distance the bolt protrudes from the lock. Common sizes are ¼", ½", and 1". Presumably, the bigger the throw the more secure the lock. On wooden doors, however, this is questionable. Few wooden doors can resist a well-placed kick from a determined criminal. On a steel buck door, however, it may be good.

Some deadbolt locks are made of cast steel and these are the easiest to drill through, a favorite criminal entry method. Others, however, have a hardened steel core or rod inside and can't be drilled through without great effort.

Modern deadlocks are mortised in the door; that is, recessed in a cavity in the edge. Old style deadbolts are available and these are mounted on the surface of the door.

Another type of deadbolt does not have a bolt throw but rather horizontal rings on it through which a bolt engages vertically. Finally, there is the jimmyproof deadbolt. A burglar can drill out the cylinder on this, but unlike normal mechanisms he cannot then stick a screwdriver or other tool in it to turn the latch. A little spring-activated plate gets in the way.

It is said that there is no lock that can bar entry to a determined criminal. This is no doubt true, but a lock that can frustrate entry can make the burglar give up. Perhaps the best of this type is the Fox police lock. This has a metal part on the door into which a thick metal rod is leaned and locked; the other end of the rod is mounted in a metal flange cup recessed in the floor. To open it by pushing the door, someone would literally have to bend the metal rod. This is when someone is home and can lock the rod in position at the top. However, according to an ex-burglar this lock can be defeated if it is not in the deadlock position, something you can only set when you go out. The company does make a special accessory to guard against this.

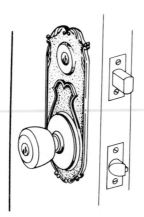

This lock has a regular cylinder lock on the bottom but a deadbolt on top. The turning lever inside is used to flip the deadlock.

Jimmyproof deadlock mounted on surface of door is from Segal. If the cylinder is wrenched out, the burglar would normally be able to turn the bolt with a screwdriver. This lock, however, has a shutter guard inside that snaps over the hole and prevents that from happening.

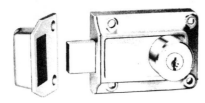

Another type of deadlock has lock cylinders on both sides and can only be operated with a key.

Replacing a Lock

Locks come with complete installation instructions. Most replacement types can be installed in the hole housing the old lock. When shopping for a replacement, the key consideration is its "backset"—the distance from the edge of the door to the middle of the knob or handle. The vast majority of locks, interior and exterior, are 2⅜" backset and most are installed in a 2⅛" hole, some in a 1¾" hole. If the hold is backset 2⅜" but only has a 1¾" hole, you can simply enlarge it. Just clamp wood over the hole and use one of the many specially sized lock boring bits available.

Some locks have a backset of 5". Quickset is a popular brand. For this you'll have to get a new bolt. Another manufacturer, Schlage, has a link that goes between the bolt and the lock.

Replacement Parts

Parts on locks are usually interchangeable. One way to save here is to keep good parts from locks that are otherwise useless. This is why it is a good idea to hang onto a lock even though it no longer works properly. If you take the lock apart you'll be able to see how the parts go together. Replacement shouldn't be difficult.

Manufacturers also sell replacement parts for their particular brand and brands of other companies. These are usually available at large hardware stores. Or you can write the manufacturer for outlets near you. The maker's name is usually on the lock.

BUYING HINTS

Door locks come in a wide variety of styles—everything from fancy filigree with a gold finish to the standard plain brass-plated type. Prices can vary widely too, anywhere from $5 to $150. Chances, are, however, that you will not necessarily get a better lock if you just buy style. If you pay more for the standard brass-plated lock, then chances are you'll get a better buy.

Hardware stores and lumberyards do not usually carry a wide selection. However, you can ask to see a catalog, pick out a style, then have the dealer order it for you or ask to be referred to a wholesale outlet where you can see the locks and then ask the dealer to order one for you or buy it yourself.

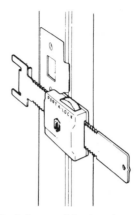

This lock is portable, handy to take to a motel to lock a door that has an inadequate lock.

Fox Police Lock

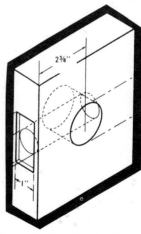

The prime consideration in shopping for a lock is the backset—the distance from the edge of the door to the middle of the knob or handle. Most locks have 2⅜" backset and go in a 2⅛" or 1¼" hole.

Boring Bit

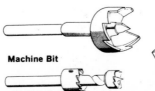

Machine Bit

Boring Bit

Combination Machine Bit

If a lock hole needs modifications there is a variety of bits available for modifying holes, as shown here.

Drapery Hardware

There are two main kinds of drapery hardware: rods and traverse rods. In the first case the drapery simply hangs from the rod. If the draperies are closed and you want to open them, you push them apart with your hands. With a traverse rod you pull on a cord that is connected to a mechanism that pulls both draperies apart at the same time.

Rods are available in a variety of styles and colors—mostly decorative brass. The commonest rod is the exposed type where the draperies hang with the rod in full view. A concealed rod is also available.

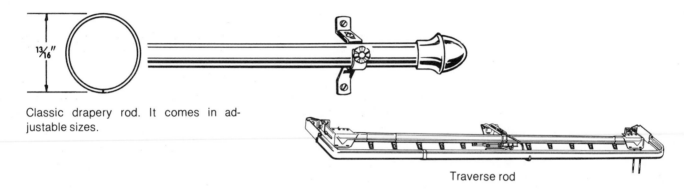

Classic drapery rod. It comes in adjustable sizes.

Traverse rod

Drapery rods are adjustable. They come with 48″ to 60″ adjustment or 24″ to 48″ or other parameters, but the important thing is that they are adjustable. In figuring what you need, you should calculate the application of the draperies—where they'll be used, the overall dimension of the window frame, and the dimensions inside the window frame. Once you know these dimensions, you shouldn't have any trouble getting hardware.

Another useful drapery rod is spring activated. You can telescope the sections together, place it inside a window well, and it will expand and stay there by spring tension.

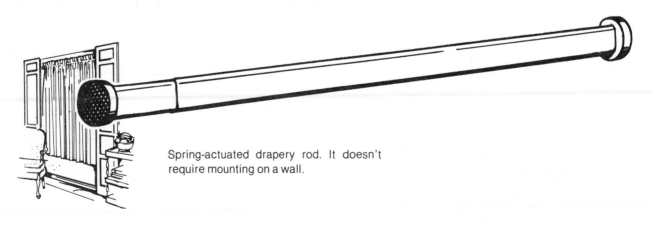

Spring-actuated drapery rod. It doesn't require mounting on a wall.

Kits

Installing drapery hardware is greatly simplified by the fact that the basic hardware—regular or traverse rods—comes in packaged form with all the necessary fasteners and complete instructions for installing it. Hanging accessories for the rods must be matched, but these are readily available. For example, for round rods there are rings that slip over the rod and on which the draperies are hung. These must be of slightly larger diameter than the rod. For traverse rods there are pins that hook onto the hangers on the traverse rod.

METAL CAFE RING WITH EYELET

Drawer Hardware

Drawer hardware consists of two kinds: the track or slides that the drawer moves on and the knobs or pulls. As with other types of products, the best bet when replacing drawer hardware is to remove the mechanism and show it to your dealer. Manufacturers vary their products greatly. The key is to have enough clearance on the sides of the drawer so that it can slide freely. If the hardware is too wide—or too narrow—it won't work well.

Tracks and Slides

Drawer hardware may ride on wheels linked with track in the center, or it may have the track and wheel arrangement on the sides. Some hardware has a stop so that you cannot pull the drawer all the way out, while other types—called full extension—allow you to pull the drawer all the way without sagging. This latter type can come in handy when you want complete access to the drawer's contents.

Another type of drawer hardware is made by the Roll-eez Company. These are basically small plastic rollers that are nailed or screwed to the drawer and to the compartment. They come in many different arrangements for different types of drawers. Roll-eez, unlike the track-wheel-type hardware, can be used to get a balky drawer working properly. The same company makes plastic pieces that function like the rollers.

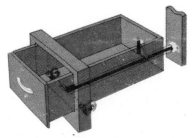

Some drawers are center mounted, as shown.

Other drawers are mounted on hardware, which itself is mounted on the bottom of a piece of furniture, such as a desk.

23

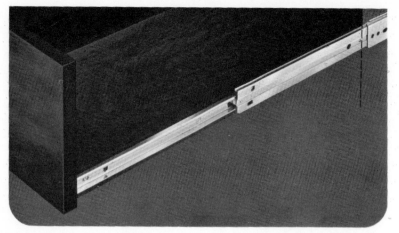

Full extension hardware allows drawer to be pulled all the way out of the cabinet (dotted line is cabinet front) for easy access to the contents. Ones shown (from Grant) can support fifty pounds of items in a drawer.

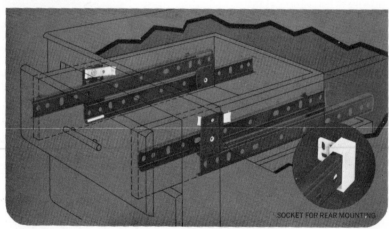

SOCKET FOR REAR MOUNTING

Hardware here only allows partial extension of drawer.

1. "N"   **2.** "N"   FRONT OF CABINET   "N"   **3.** "M"   BACK VIEW OF DRAWER

Roll-eez drawer rollers can be installed on existing or new drawers to make them work more easily. They come in forms and the selection is based on the type of drawer and cabinet construction—with or without dust shelves, side guides, etc. Show a sketch of the drawer-cabinet construction to your dealer to ensure getting the correct set.

LEFT CORNER GUIDE   RIGHT CORNER GUIDE

FRONT OF CABINET

Plastic guides (from Roll-eez) are part of set which makes drawers easier to operate in humid weather when wood fibers swell and it is difficult to operate drawer.

Knobs and Pulls

These items are available in a great variety of styles and sizes. For more information, see page 5.

24

Framing Fasteners

A number of companies make fasteners for framing that can be used in place of nails and screws. The devices, made of either 16- or 18-gauge zinc-coated metal, have predrilled holes. Essentially, you set the device between two framing members and drive nails (or screws) through the holes to lock the members together.

A couple of points should be made before discussing these fasteners. First, they make framing connections stronger; indeed, a number are designed to join members so that they can resist hurricane-force winds. However, in many areas of the country, hurricanes (and similar meteorological happenings) are not a problem. So the do-it-yourselfer should evaluate carefully whether the extra strength is going to justify the cost, which is a lot more than just nails. Second, though the fasteners are accepted by most local building codes, this may not be the case in your particular community. As with any building project, your plans should first be checked against local building codes (or risk having to disassemble the job later).

Joist and Beam Hangers

Carpenters use these devices widely and swear by them. The Panel Clip Company calls theirs joist clips, the Teco Company calls theirs U-grips. Another company, F. D. Kees, calls theirs joist hangers. They are available in various sizes, as are most of the fasteners. For example, Teco makes them to accommodate everything from 2″ × 4″ to 4″ × 4″ joists and beams.

One advantage of joist and beam hangers is that they eliminate a lot of work. In standard joist framing, joist ends must be notched and rested on a ledger strip that is nailed to the box framing joist. The hangers are simply set in place on the box joist and nailed. The end of the joist is then slid into the hanger, and nails are driven through the hanger to secure it. The other advantage is strength. When joists or beams are notched, their load-carrying capacity is reduced.

Another useful fastener is made for anchoring posts to masonry. One advantage here is that the post rides on the device off the concrete, which reduces the chances of rot and termite attack. And, as opposed to the setting of regular posts and bolts in concrete, where bolts and the corresponding holes in the post bottoms must be right on the money, the devices (and posts) may be moved after the concrete is set. In other words, misaligned posts may be realigned.

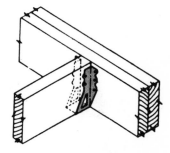

Carpenters swear by joist hangers. They let you fasten the joists in place without having to notch the ends for securing to the ledger strip on the box joist (double member shown).

Fastener shown is for anchoring posts to concrete. The post end rests on top of a U-shaped piece with a hole in it, so that there is no direct contact with the concrete. Fasteners may also be adjusted to align posts if bolts in the concrete are misaligned.

Fasteners for beams let you do a neat job without toenailing vertical and horizontal members together.

Right-angle fasteners are available for eliminating the need to toenail studs in place, a problem for inexperienced do-it-yourselfers.

Another useful framing fastener is that used to connect posts and the horizontal members that ride on them. The fastener is nailed to the post and then the horizontal member slipped into it and nailed in place, thus eliminating toenailing. Teco calls their product post caps, Panel Clip dubs theirs beam clips.

To simplify fence construction, there are fence brackets. These are basically metal boxes with two sides missing. The box is screwed (or nailed) to a fence post, and the rail end is slid into place. No nailing, screwing, or notching is necessary, but the rails can be permanently screwed or nailed to the hangers if you wish. This slide-in feature also allows you to remove entire fence sections for such tasks as cutting the lawn, painting, or removing snow. The brackets may also be used for nailing privacy screens onto the porch, patio, or carport; they have indoor applications as well.

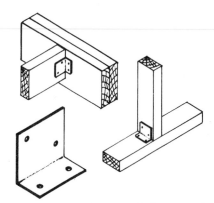

Angles are mainly used for securing studs. If you're not experienced at toenailing, these may be for you.

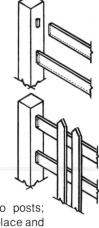

Fence brackets are secured to posts; then the fence rails are slid into place and either secured or left loose.

Truss Fasteners

To make a roof truss properly, members are joined with nailed and glued-on plywood gussets. Fasteners are designed to eliminate the necessity of gussets. These fasteners are basically flat metal plates, either with holes for nailing or with built-in barbs. Teco calls their nailed type truss plates. These are placed over the members to be joined and are nailed in place. Barbed versions, which are hammered in place, may require a special hammering tool.

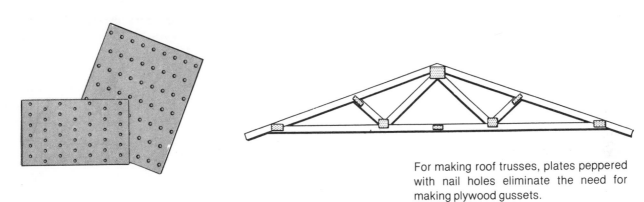

For making roof trusses, plates peppered with nail holes eliminate the need for making plywood gussets.

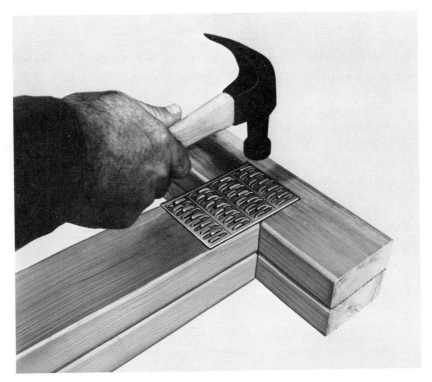

On the fastener shown, the barbs are banged down with a hammer, which locks the members together.

Other Framing Fasteners

There is a variety of other fasteners you may want to examine. These include clips for joining roof sheathing, straps to tie various members together, and truss plates (panel clips) for assembling garage door headers.

It should be noted that in most cases individual fasteners may be used for a variety of framing jobs, even though they may have been primarily designed for one. For example, the right angles for installing studs may be used for other jobs. Teco shows in its literature six different uses for its joist hangers. It all depends on how you place the fasteners. Also, most can be bent, allowing additional use flexibility.

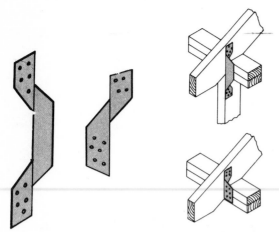

Some hangers may be too strong for your needs. For example, the ones shown tie rafters to the plate in one case *(lower right-hand detail)* and to the plate and studs in another *(upper right-hand detail)*. This type of fastening can keep your roof on in a hurricane.

BUYING TIPS

Framing fasteners are available in small packages, loose, and in bulk cartons. Whichever way you buy them, the manufacturer supplies the nails. Bulk packages may run twenty-five to fifty pieces to the carton. Buying in bulk is by far the most economical; you can expect to save roughly fifty percent over small packages. Since fasteners are not cheap (for example, a pair of Teco joist and beam hangers, complete with nails, costs at this writing around $1.50 or so), it's something to keep in mind.

If you do buy bulk, make sure that the carton the fasteners comes in also contains the nails. Insiders in the industry say that many times cartons are opened and nails sold off for other purposes.

Framing fasteners are available in home centers, lumberyards, and hardware stores. Your best bet in terms of selection will probably be the lumberyard, since it is the lumberyard's business to sell wood, and that's what these fasteners are for.

Gutter

Gutter is made of five different materials: wood, copper, vinyl, galvanized metal, and aluminum. But for all practical purposes only vinyl, galvanized metal, and aluminum are really do-it-yourself materials.

Wood

Wood gutters are still available, but if you plan to install them yourself be aware of a number of disadvantages. For one thing, wood gutter (usually made of fir) is very expensive. It's also heavy, weighing up to five and six times more than metal gutter. Finally, every couple of years the inside must be coated with pitch to protect the wood from rot.

On the positive side, it is good looking, and you can install unjointed–seamless–pieces on your house, since it is available in lengths up to 50'. The average home would probably not need longer pieces. The point here is that wherever a gutter is joined, it is susceptible to leaks. Check lumberyards for wood gutter.

Copper

This gutter is still available, but it is not much used anymore. Reason? It is prohibitively expensive. It comes in standard lengths of 10'; joints must be soldered.

Vinyl

This is polyvinyl chloride. It comes in 5″ size (measuring from the front lip to the back piece) and is available in varying lengths (10', 16', 21', 32') in only one color, white. Vinyl gutter can be cut easily. Wherever connections are made, special connectors are used; these are cemented and fastened in place.

Vinyl is not susceptible to rust, corrosion, rotting, peeling, and the like. Its big bugaboo, however, is that in cold weather it can crack due to expansion and contraction. For this reason, people who live in cold climates should think carefully about its advisability.

Galvanized Metal

Galvanized steel gutter comes plain and in various baked-enamel finishes. Standard length is 10' (it is also available 20' long), and it may be had in widths of 4″ or 5″. The 4″ size is to be avoided: It simply doesn't have much water-carrying ability (4″ is a favorite for home builders who want to save money). It is available in standard K style and half-round shapes. Galvan-

INSTALLATION TIPS

There are a couple of things to be especially aware of when installing gutter.

All gutter must pitch on the house so that when the water stops flowing through it, not a single drop is left. In doing this, many people (even professionals) make a logical mistake: They assume that the house is level and establish their pitch line off that. The fact is that a house is hardly ever level. To obtain proper pitch, you must establish a level line independent of the house and then establish a pitch line off that.

If you install aluminum gutters, do so with Pop (blind) rivets rather than sheet metal screws.

Nails used with hangers should go into the rafter ends, not just the fascia board. Lifting up the shingles that overlap the edge of the house will ordinarily show you where the ends are located. Some houses are framed so that there are solid framing members all along the edge of the house; this is just as good as rafter ends for anchoring.

Finally, you should fully grasp the importance of gutters on your house. Gutters that have been properly installed will carry away thousands of gallons of water each year. But if they're not installed correctly or if they leak, water can spill over (especially when the gutters ice up), saturate the foundation, and seep into the basement. It's safe to say that incorrectly installed or leaky gutters are the number one cause of damp and wet basements.

2 x 2 – 19 Ga.

4 x 4 – 23 Ga.

8 x 8 – 27 Ga.

Hardware cloth comes in various meshes. The smaller the mesh, the greater the gauge.

Hardware Cloth

Hardware cloth is a type of rugged screening that can be very useful around the home. It is simple to work with. It can be cut with tin snips and has some flexibility. It is sold by the foot in rolls of various widths ranging from 2' to 4'.

The galvanized material comes in various meshes, commonly 2×2, 4×4, 8×8. This refers to the number of squares to the inch. To find this, just multiply the numbers: in 2×2, for example, there are 4 squares to the inch, in 4×4 there are 16, and so forth. As the number of squares per inch increases, the gauge of the metal decreases. So, for example, the 2×2 is 19 gauge, the 4×4 is 23 gauge, and the 8×8 is 27 gauge (wire sizes get smaller as the gauge numbers get higher).

One of the main uses of hardware cloth is as a sifter—sifting sand, cement, topsoil, and the like. The fine material drops through, while the stones remain on the cloth. Another popular and good use is for pet cages. My son, for example, built a gerbil cage with it that has lasted for years. You can also think of it as screening wherever you want extra security. It is often used to keep squirrels, birds, or bats out of various house or barn sections.

Poultry Netting

Poultry netting, also called poultry fence, is a large mesh (commonly in squares of 1″ and 2″) galvanized wire that comes in heights up to 6′ and up to 50′ lengths. This allows for a pretty high setup should you need it. It is sold by the foot in hardware stores.

Poultry netting is not nearly as strong as hardware cloth, but it doesn't cost as much; indeed, it's cheap. Most people use poultry fence for protection against the encroachment of small animals, such as rabbits, on their property. A favorite use is to mount it on a split-rail fence to keep a dog confined. This is a much less costly solution for confining the pet than installing something like chain-link fence.

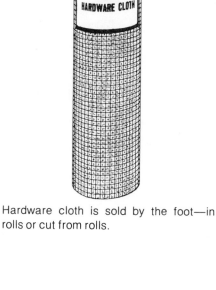

Hardware cloth is sold by the foot—in rolls or cut from rolls.

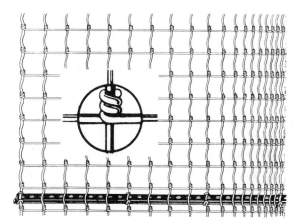

Poultry netting showing a close-up of the way strands are connected

Bed Guard

Bed guard is a short wire fencing that is used for protection against the encroachment of rabbits and other small animals on flower beds. It comes galvanized, but can also be obtained in colors—white, green, and sometimes yellow—so it can add a decorative accent.

It is 14″ high and comes in rolls of 25′. Mounting is simple: You just press the projecting wires at the bottom into the soil.

Bed guard. It comes in colors.

Hinges

Hinges come in a seemingly endless variety of types, but keeping in mind the following facts should eliminate some of the confusion.

Many companies specify that hinges are "handed"—that is, designed to go on either the left or right hand of the door. In some cases the left hand is considered left as you view the door opening from the outside of the house; in others it is from the inside. This can get very complicated, and the simple fact is that unless you are involved in a very special situation, you don't need to know the hands, because hinges are interchangeable. All you need to do is turn them over, and they become left-handed or right-handed, as required.

Different types of hinges come in various sizes; in the very small sizes they would be used on cabinet doors. In selecting any hinge for a door, there is a variety of data one should know: door thickness, weight, and clearance. But a long-time engineering trick makes it simpler: If the hinge seems to be in proportion to the door it's going on, use it. For example, if you are hanging an exterior door, you won't use tiny hinges, nor would you use extra large ones. We are all generally familiar with hinge size and your own judgment should suffice.

Actually, it would be extremely difficult to select hinges that are too small, simply because hinges are tremendously strong— eight or more times, generally, stronger than the job they are called upon to do. As a rule of thumb, though, for a normal-weight interior sash 1⅜″ thick or hollow-core flush (flat and smooth door use 1 pair of 3½″ × 3½″ butt hinges; for a solid door 1⅜″ thick use 1½ pairs of 3½″ × 3½″; for a door 1¾″ thick use 1 pair of 4″ × 4″ butts; for a solid-core door 1¾″ thick use 1½ pairs of 4″ × 4″ butts; and for door blinds 1⅛″ thick use 1½ pairs of 3″ × 3″ butts. The thickness of the door dictates the size of the hinges and the weight and the number of hinges.

Butt Hinge

The butt hinge is commonly used on interior and exterior doors because it is neat looking. It consists of two rectangular leaves with screw holes. The leaves are joined by a pin or metal rod. Withdraw this pin and the leaves will separate, handy for when you want to take down the door. Both leaves are mortised, or recessed: one into the edge of the door, the other in the jamb, or door framework. When the door is closed, the leaves meet, or butt together, with only the pin showing.

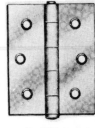

Butt hinge

T-**Hinge**

The T-hinge, as the name suggests, is shaped like the letter T. The horizontal part of the T goes on the door frame, while the vertical part is screwed to the door.

This hinge is flush mounted—not recessed into the door—and you'd use the plain kind where you care more about function than about good looks. T-hinges are commonly used on garage doors, to hinge chest lids, and for other utility jobs. Ornamental T-hinges are also available.

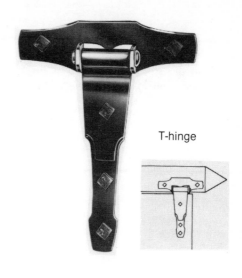

T-hinge

Strap Hinge

This is another hinge for utility rather than looks. It consists of two long narrow leaves of equal size extending from a single knuckle. Strap hinges come in various sizes, both large and small; but the length of the leaves militates against their being mounted on a normal doorjamb. Rather, they are the kind of hinge to use where you have a lid of some sort that you want hinged in the center. In marine use, for example, you'll find strap hinges on fish box lids. When small fish are caught, either side of the lid can be lifted and the fish tossed in the box. When a large fish is caught, the entire lid can be lifted off and the fish placed in the box. For around the home you might use a strap hinge on an outdoor storage box.

Strap hinges are commonly available in the same finishes (plain and galvanized steel) as T-hinges. You can also get them in bronze, but these are ordinarily for boats.

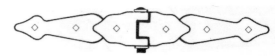

Strap hinges also come in ornamental styles.

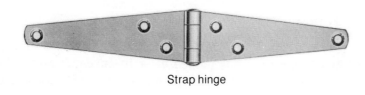

Strap hinge

Gate Hinge

The gate hinge has two parts: an L-shaped lag screw that screws into the fence post and a leaf with a knurled nut that fits over the L of the first part and is screwed to the gate. Gate hinges were specifically designed so that they could be easily attached to round posts, but they can be mounted on square posts as well.

While they are theoretically available in a variety of sizes, you'll usually find them in sizes of either 5″ or 6″.

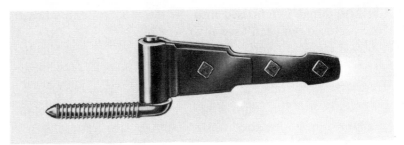

Gate hinge. Screwing or unscrewing it raises the door for leveling and clearance.

An advantage of a gate hinge is that if the gate is hung and it is not straight, the hinge can be adjusted to compensate: Just lift the gate off the hinge, turn the lag-screw part of the hinge, and rehang the door.

Special-Purpose Hinges

A number of special-purpose hinges are of particular interest.

Double-acting hinge

One type of hinge is for dividers that you want to fold in both directions or that you want to fold flat for storage. This is called the double-acting hinge. It comes in two forms; one type has two leaves and knuckles and is somewhat loose jointed because both leaves can open at once. The other is more complicated but is designed to permit the doors to fold either way; they allow the door to open only one edge at a time.

Soss Hinge

This type of hinge (for cabinets, folding doors, and shutters but not regular doors) is named after its inventor and is for situations where you want a hinge that is completely concealed.

The Soss hinge will result in a completely concealed hinge—but it's difficult to install. Mortises are drilled and the hinges slipped into place and tightened.

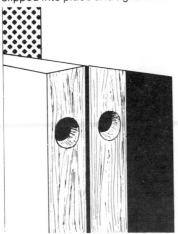

The Soss hinge is mortised into the door edges, and when the door is closed, you can't see any part of it.

Soss hinges are very strong, but they are very difficult to install. There is simply no room for error; they must be lined up directly opposite each other right on the money. They are also expensive.

Piano, or Continuous, Hinge

Another name for this type of hinge is the continuous hinge, but is commonly called a piano hinge because this is what it is normally used on. It is a long hinge with very narrow leaves and many screw holes. It was designed for a piano because it combines strength with good looks. (It is commonly available in brass finish.) You couldn't use strap or other hinges on a piano lid without detracting from its looks.

Piano hinges are available in various sizes. They are especially good where the material is thin and strength and good looks are required.

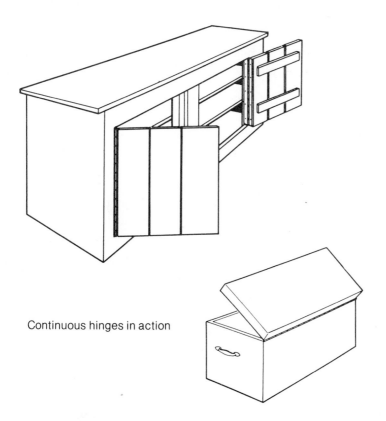

Continuous hinges in action

Miscellaneous Products

A number of important products don't lend themselves to easy classification. Following, in no particular order, is a grab bag of these.

Sawhorse Brackets

A number of manufacturers make these. Essentially, they are pieces of stamped metal with holes in them for screws and are intended to accept and support tables or sawhorses. There are lightweight and heavyweight types. Larson, for example, makes brackets to accept 2″ × 2″ and 2″ × 4″ lumber boards for legs plus a 2″ × 4″ crosspiece, but they also offer heavy-duty brackets that will accept 1″ × 4″ boards for legs with a 2″ × 4″ crosspiece. The brackets come with the screws and nails necessary for attaching them.

Metal Folding Legs

Also available are metal folding legs in various sizes for light- or heavy-duty applications. These usually come in bright metal and black finishes.

Hasps

These range in styles and sizes. The length of the slotted part generally ranges from 2¼″ to 6¼″, with staples (the part with the ring for the lock) of proportionate sizes and hasp widths 1″ to 2″.

Safety hasps are a home security device. When closed, the slotted part conceals the screws that attach it to the door. Since an intruder can't get at the screws, he or she can't remove the hasp, at least with a screwdriver.

Also for security, there is a hasp that is heavy duty and has four regular screw holes but also a square hole for insertion of a $\frac{5}{16}$″ carriage bolt, which, of course, would make removal difficult.

Another safety hasp is expressly designed for use on chests, sliding doors, and the like. It has an upturned end, and when mounted, the screws are concealed, making removal difficult.

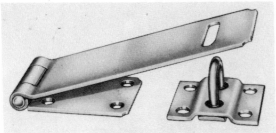

This is called a safety hasp, because it's more difficult for a burglar to beat. When the slotted part is in place, the screws that secure the hasp are covered with metal.

Decorative Hasps

Smaller hasps are also available for decorative use—on baskets, boxes, chests, cabinets, and the like. Stanley makes a slotted strap type 1⅝″ long that is available in bright plate brass. Larger sizes are also available.

Hasps are available both loose and carded. In most cases they are packaged with screws for mounting.

Trapdoor Rings

A trapdoor ring consists of a steel pad on which a handle, called a bail, is mounted. The pad has holes for accepting screws. A standard size is a 3″ × 3½″ plate with a bail diameter of 2⅛″. It's a good idea to get one where the ring lies in a recess in the pad so that no one will trip over it if it's located in a well-traveled area of the house. Trapdoor rings are generally available in japanned steel or zinc plated.

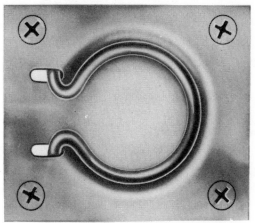

Trapdoor ring. It's a good idea to get one with the bail (handle) recessed so that people can't trip over it.

Chest Handles

Closely related to the trapdoor ring is the chest handle. It has a plate for mounting and differs from the trapdoor ring in the size of the bail and the pad, both of which are larger. For example, the trapdoor ring Stanley shows in its catalogue has an inside diameter of 1½″; the same company's chest handle bail has an inside diameter of 2⅞″. The reason, of course, is that you are likely to lift a chest handle more frequently than a trapdoor ring, so the extra size is provided for a more comfortable grip. There are also chest handles available with tubular shape, which make gripping even easier.

One other type of chest handle has no holes for mounting with screws but a solid steel plate that is designed to be welded to a chest or box.

If you have a particularly narrow box, chest handles may be obtained with narrow plates and large bails. For example, Stanley has one whose plate is 3⁷⁄₁₆″ long but less than 1½″ wide.

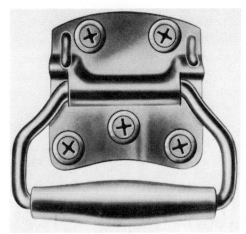

Chest handle. Its bail must be larger than that of a trapdoor ring because it's used more.

Braces

There are some items, such as tables and chairs, that take particularly hard abuse. For strengthening the joints between

Corner brace

members of these and other items there are braces in various shapes.

The corner brace, an L-shaped piece of steel with screw holes for mounting, comes in sizes that range from 1″ long and ½″ wide to 8″ long and more than 1″ wide. As the sizes get larger (over 5″), the screw holes are normally staggered rather than being in one line.

Corner braces are particularly good for strengthening and supporting wood frames such as box and chair corners and wood window and door frames.

T-Plates and Flat Corner Irons

T-plates, as the name implies, are made in the shape of the letter T, with both the horizontal and the vertical members of the T the same length. A common use for T-plates is for joining horizontal and vertical wood-frame screen sections.

Flat corner irons also come in various sizes, both large and small. These are L-shaped, with screw holes for mounting, and are good for connecting frame pieces at the corner on the surfaces.

Both T-plates and corner irons are available in brass-plated finishes as well as zinc plated.

T-plate

T-plate in action (corner brace also shown)

Corner iron

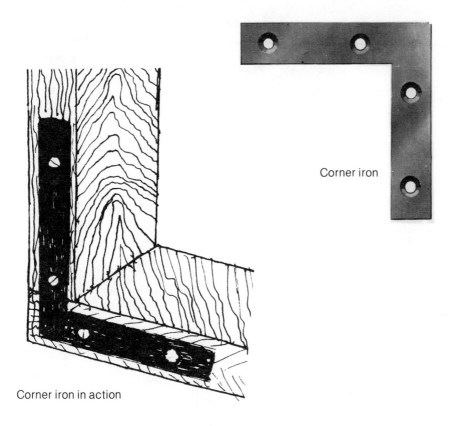

Corner iron in action

Mending Plates

These are probably the most widely used braces of all. They are available brass plated as well as in wrought steel and zinc, and come in a range of sizes. They have many different applications, from mending wood screen and storm sash to fixing furniture.

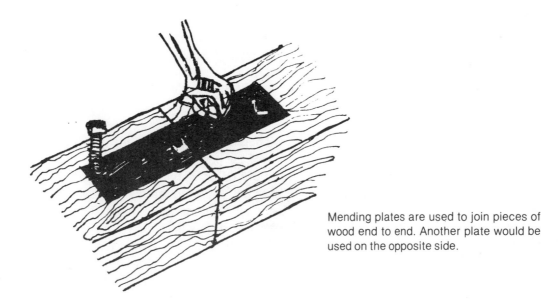

Mending plate

Mending plates are used to join pieces of wood end to end. Another plate would be used on the opposite side.

Corner braces are used for reinforcing metal-frame screens.

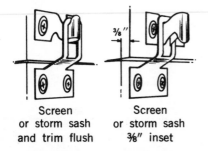

Screen or storm sash and trim flush | Screen or storm sash ⅜" inset

Screen and storm sash hangers

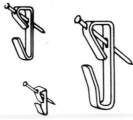

Picture hooks are simple, useful items. They are driven in the wall with a hammer and can hold varying weights, depending on size. They needn't be mounted in studs.

Corner Braces

Corner braces are used for reinforcing screens with metal channels. These come carded, with one mounted on each corner. They are also designed for use on wood-frame screen doors.

Turnbuttons

A turnbutton is mounted on the frame of a screen or storm sash and retains the screen or sash. These are available in several sizes and are either galvanized or zinc plated.

Turnbutton

Screen and Storm Sash Hangers

There are a few kinds of these available. One is for screens or storms that hang flush with the window casing; the other type is for screens or storm windows where the top is inset from the casing.

Storm Sash Adjuster

If you want to open a storm sash only to a certain point, use an adjuster. This is basically a folding leg, one end of which is attached to the window frame, the other to the storm sash. The sash can be opened to any degree desired and then set by a friction adjustment.

Picture Hooks

There are many different devices for hanging pictures, but one of the best is the nail-on type. This is available in both plain and ornamental styles, with common capacities for holding 10-, 20-, and 50-pound framed pictures or paintings. The device is installed by hammering a nail at an angle through a hole in the fastener; it can be used on any type of wall. The picture or painting is then hung from the device.

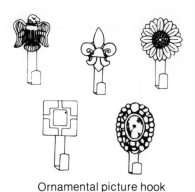

Ornamental picture hook

Chair brace

Speedy Rivets

These fasteners (Speedy is a brand name) are for joining various types of soft materials such as canvas, or leather and canvas. To install one, a hole is punched in the material and the riveted portion of the fastener slipped through; the other section is then placed over it, and the rivet is whacked with a hammer. The material is joined. Some kinds of Speedy rivets require a special clamping tool for joining instead of a hammer.

T-nut fastener

Tee-Nut Fasteners

A situation may arise where you need a threaded core in wood for a machine screw. For example, you may want to join a pair of 2 × 4's this way. For this kind of job there is the Tee-Nut fastener. It is mounted in a drilled hole in one of the boards; a machine screw is then passed through a drilled hole in the other 2 × 4 and into the threaded core.

Speedy rivet

Pop Rivets

In the past, sheet metal screws were used to connect gutter sections and fittings. Today the blind rivet gun—more popularly known by the brand name of one gun the Pop Rivet Tool (USM)—is used extensively. It is faster and just as secure. To use it, the shank of a rivet is stuck into the nose of the gun; the rivet itself, protrudes. The rivet is then stuck through the hole and the tool handles are squeezed; and the rivet compresses, locking the parts together. When the rivet is fully compressed, the shank is clipped off by the tool.

The beauty of this tool is that it installs blind rivets. You don't need access to the two sides of an item in order to be able

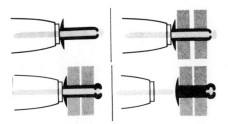

Steps in setting a blind rivet: The rivet is stuck in the nose of the gun and passed through a drilled hole; the handles on the gun are squeezed until the rivet is compressed. The rivet gun automatically clips off the shank.

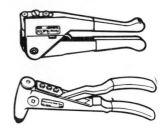

Rivet guns may be consumer type, top, or professional.

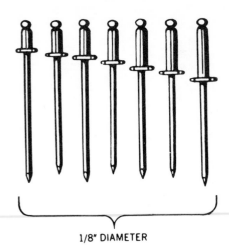

1/8″ DIAMETER

Blind rivets come in various diameters and lengths. The hole should be just big enough to allow the rivet head through, and the rivet should be deep enough that when compressed, it grips both parts together tightly.

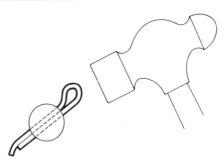

Cotter pin. One leg is longer than the other in order to permit it to be gripped and bent back by pliers.

to rivet it, as you would, say, if you wanted to pull two parts together with a nut and bolt.

Many metal jobs may be done this way: fixing toys, bikes, appliances, and other things. The tool can also be used for joining fabric.

Rivets are available in a variety of sizes. When using them, two things should be remembered: The hole drilled (punched) must be the same diameter as the rivet and, secondly, you must use a rivet that is large (deep) enough to join whatever it is you want joined.

Other miscellaneous hardware items are also available. Some of the ones you will be more likely to use are shown in the illustrations below.

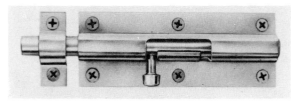

Door bolt

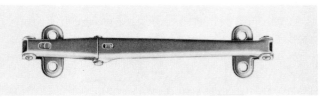

Table leaf brace

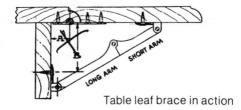

Table leaf brace in action

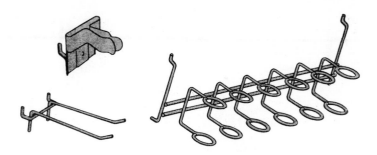

Pegboard hangers. These are hooked into a pegboard for holding shelves, bottles, and so on. There are numerous kinds.

This is for insertion into a door for viewing visitors.

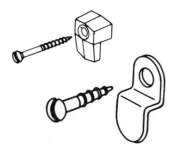

These fasteners are screwed to a door and grip a mirror by the edges.

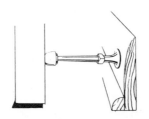

Doorstop. This comes in various sizes and finishes.

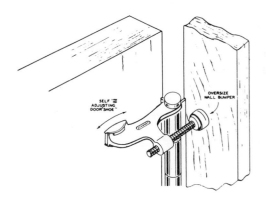

This doorstop keeps a door from opening all the way.

Various-size clamps have many uses, from gardening projects to securing various items. They are usually made of stainless steel.

Nails

Nails are generally available in sizes that range from 1″ to 6″ long; as the nail gets longer, the diameter gets correspondingly thicker. When speaking of size, nails are referred to by weight and number. Weight is expressed by the letter *d* and stands for pennyweight (the way nails used to be sold), with sizes running from 2d (1″) to 60d (6″).

There are many different kinds of nails available, some of which can serve a variety of purposes, while others are more specialized in their use (roofing nails, for example). There should be no reason why you can't get a nail ideally suited to the job at hand.

Common Nails and Finishing Nails

As the name implies, this is a very common nail and good for a wide variety of fastening purposes. Most people use them for general construction-type work; framing and the like. The common nail comes in a wide range of sizes and has a large, flat head that provides a good-size hitting surface and acts like a washer in holding the nail in place. Common sizes are 4d, 6d, 8d, 10d.

A variation on the common nail is the box nail. It is like the common type but thinner and good to use where a thicker common style might split the wood.

The finishing nail is perhaps the second most popular nail. It is thinner than the common type, but its main feature is its small head. The nail is designed for assembling work where you don't want the nailheads to show. After the nail is driven flush with the surface, a nail set is used to sink (technically known as countersink) the cupped head beneath the surface of the wood, and the cavity above it is filled with wood putty. When sanded and finished, it is difficult to determine where the nail is. In the very small sizes, usually up to 1½″ long, finishing nails are called brads.

Some common nails come with threaded shanks.

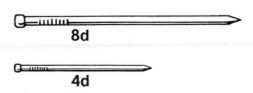

Finishing nails (actual size)

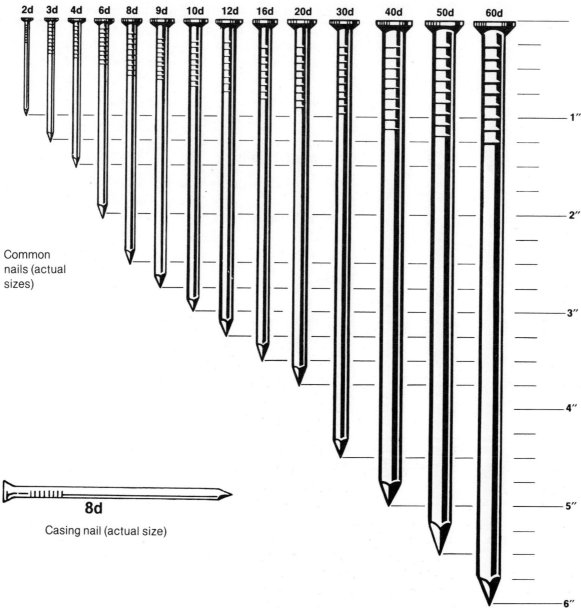

Common
nails (actual
sizes)

2d 3d 4d 6d 8d 9d 10d 12d 16d 20d 30d 40d 50d 60d

1″
2″
3″
4″
5″
6″

8d

Casing nail (actual size)

A variation on the finishing nail is the casing nail. This gets
its name from its primary use on case molding, or rough trim.
It is thicker and stronger than the regular finishing nail and
though appearance is similar it has a flat rather than cupped
head. As such it is not designed to be countersunk below the
surface and the hole filled with putty or other filler, but is
driven flush with the surface and then simply painted over.

Common and finishing nails generally come without a
finish—they're just plain steel. But both types are available in
galvanized, either coated or hot dipped. The latter process
leaves the surface of the nail with a rough finish that is not only
superior, in terms of weather resistance over the coated nail,

but the roughness allows the nail to grip better. Both common and finishing nails are also available in a blued finish. These are not rustproof; rust resistant would be a more accurate way to describe them. (Indeed, hardware expert Warren Deming says they are blued just so that they don't rust in the box while waiting to be sold.)

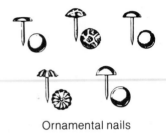

Ornamental nails

Ornamental Nails

Ornamental nails have large, fancy, oval heads and are mainly for securing upholstery. The finish is commonly either brass or chrome plated.

Tacks

These commonly come in various sizes but are usually classified by number. They are generally available in a blued finish or copper; copper tacks are impervious to weather. While the latter are commonly used in marine applications, they also have good uses around the home, such as for securing webbing to patio furniture.

Tacks are usually called carpet tacks, which describes their main function of securing rugs and carpets to floors.

STANDARD TACK SIZES

ESTABLISHED LENGTHS OF TACKS MEASURED UNDER THE HEAD

Nos.	1	1-1/2	2	2-1/2	3	4	6	8	10	12	14	16	18	20	22	24
Ins.	3/16"	7/32"	1/4"	5/16"	3/8"	7/16"	1/2"	9/16"	5/8"	11/16"	3/4"	13/16"	7/8"	15/16"	1"	1-1/8"

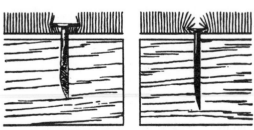

The advantage of a small head carpet tack

Specialized Nails and Fasteners

Roofing nails. A roofing nail has an extralarge head and a barbed shank. It is designed to hold shingles, roofing paper, and the like to roofs without damaging the material (the large head prevents the roofing from pulling loose through the nailhead). They come in various sizes, with the most common available ⅜″, ⅞″, and 1¼″. The size you use will depend on the thickness of the material being installed.

Drywall nails. For securing Sheetrock, also known as drywall and plasterboard, there is the drywall nail. It has a countersunk (depressed in the center) head and a partially barbed shank; the barbed part is down near the end; when the nail passes through the drywall, the part that bites into the stud grabs fast. It is available in a few sizes so you can get ones deep enough to go through whatever thickness of Sheetrock you are using.

The drywall nail head also dimples the paper covering on the drywall so that when a joint compound is applied, it covers the head, leaving no trace of it.

Spiral nails. This nail is also known as a drive screw. It has a spiral shank that, when you drive the nail, rotates and gives the nail a tremendous grip on the wood, probably the greatest of any nail. The nail is normally used for securing flooring, but it can be used on rough carpentry.

Masonry nails. These, too, come in a variety of sizes and lengths. The size you use depends on what you want to fasten or support.

The nail is made of tempered, case-hardened steel. It has to be; it is designed to be driven into masonry. (You must use a heavy hammer [2-pound], and it is important to wear goggles or other glasses to protect your eyes against flying masonry chips.)

A common application for the masonry nail is to hang studding on a block wall.

Panel nails. You can buy small colored nails to match the paneling you're using. This saves the job of having to countersink brads and fill depressions with wood putty. Just tap the nail in place and its head color will not be noticeable.

Staples. Carpentry staples (as opposed to the ones used for electrical wire) are U-shaped with pointed ends and are driven in place with a hammer. Points may have a variety of shapes, but most common is the slash point, in which one point is sheared

Roofing nail

Drywall nail. The head of this nail is sunk a bit so that it can be set fractionally below the surface of drywall paper covering and hidden with joint compound.

This is perhaps the most tenacious-gripping nail of all.

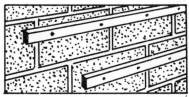
The masonry nail is capable of securing studs to masonry.

DOUBLE-HEAD SCAFFOLD

This nail is good for temporary framing. The double head lets you pull it out easily (it's sunk only to the first head).

Staple with slash point. The legs spread as it sinks.

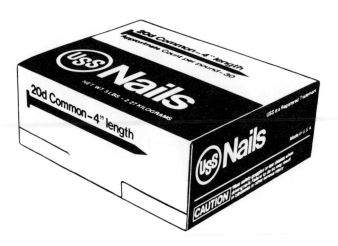

The corrugated nail is good for joining edge-to-edge boards and other work where a finishing nail would be unwieldy. Stanley makes a special tool for driving them.

Nails are ordinarily available in 1- and 5-pound boxes, but you can get 25- and 50-pound kegs. Surprisingly, the very active do-it-yourselfer can use them up quickly, so it will be a good buy.

off on an angle; the other point is also sheared off but on the reverse side of its corresponding point. The effect, when the staple is driven, is to make the legs spread, giving it better gripping action.

Staples are commonly available in galvanized finishes only, simply because they are designed for exterior use: anchoring cable, securing fencing to posts, and the like. Sizes commonly are in the ⅞″ to 1¼″ range, though much larger staples may be purchased.

Corrugated fasteners. Corrugated fasteners come in various lengths. They are small pieces of metal in corrugated form with one edge sharpened. These fasteners are strictly for joining wood edge to edge, jobs where nails would be unsuitable or difficult to use. For example, if you wanted to create a 24″-wide board and couldn't buy it in that size, you could lay two 12″ pieces edge to edge and join them with corrugated fasteners driven in from the top.

The finish of corrugated fasteners is usually blued; various sizes are available.

BUYING TIPS

You can buy certain kinds of nails carded, loose, and in brown paper bags. The common way, however, is in 1- and 5-pound boxes. The greater the quantity you buy, the more money you will save. If you expect to use a lot of nails, you can even buy 25- and 50-pound kegs (the way many contractors buy them).

INSTALLATION TIPS

When using a nail, there are a couple of points to keep in mind: When fastening two boards together, the nail should penetrate approximately three-quarters of the way through both boards. Choose a nail length accordingly. If you are working on very hard wood, there is a danger of splitting the wood with a thick nail. To avoid this, give thought to using two smaller, thinner nails. You can get the same (or better) holding power without the risk of splitting the material.

Nuts and Bolts

Nuts and bolts are for assembling things where you need great strength; where screws or nails simply aren't strong enough. There are three basic kinds of bolts that are widely used: the lag screw, the carriage bolt, and the machine bolt.

Lag Screws, Carriage Bolts, and Machine Bolts

The lag screw is for use in wood. It is partially threaded like a screw and tapered, and its head is most often square in shape but may be hexagonal.

Lag screws are very strong fasteners, and they are used mostly in the small sizes (½″ to 6″ long) for a very practical reason: They must be turned with a wrench—either an adjustable wrench or a socket wrench, which may be used on the hexagonal-headed ones. In the very large sizes they would be simply too big to turn.

You can think of a lag screw—in sizes ¼″ in diameter and up—as a screw that takes over for a regular screw when real holding power is required. It is heartily recommended that you drill pilot holes and shank holes for lag screws.

Carriage bolts got their name from the fact that they used to be the fastener for assembling horse-drawn carriages. To install one, a hole is drilled the diameter of the shank. The bolt is slipped through the hole until it reaches a point directly under the head where the shank is square. The bolt is then driven into the wood with a hammer, thereby countersinking the bolt and locking it in place so that it can't turn. A washer or nut can be threaded on the protruding end without having to hold the bolt. You can use carriage bolts in wood in operations where an exposed head is not going to be a problem (in the way).

Lag screw

Carriage bolt

Machine bolt

A machine bolt has a large square head and is installed like a carriage bolt, except that it has no square portion under the head and it must be hand held when the nuts are run on it. It comes in various sizes. Machine bolts may be used on metal and wood items. It is possible to exert good tension on a machine bolt because it is tightened with wrenches—one on the nut and another on the head.

All three kinds of bolts—machine, lag, and carriage—are available in a variety of finishes. They may be black (standard) and oiled a bit so that they don't rust in the container, and they also come galvanized—they won't rust on the job. Bolts for marine work are available at marine supplies stores in brass and stainless steel.

Lock washer. Under a bolt it grips tenaciously and keeps the bolt stationary.

Washers and Nuts

Nuts are used on machine and carriage bolts. Washers should be used on soft wood where you don't want the nut to dig into the wood or damage it. A common use is with redwood used for outdoor furniture. If a carriage or machine bolt has a tendency to work loose, use a lock washer under it. Once tightened, these washers won't move.

If you want to create greater tension on a machine or carriage bolt, use two nuts. A common use for this double-nutting is when assembling the components of a workbench, which is subject to a lot of vibration. Lock washers are also good in this situation.

In addition to the standard nuts used on carriage and machine bolts, there are a few other common ones you should know about. One is the cap nut, also called an acorn nut, which is used where looks count. Another is the wing nut, which is good if you expect to disassemble something periodically. Another useful nut has a fiber insert and is self-locking. It acts like a double nut or lock washer and provides a higher degree of tension or holding power.

Cap, or acorn, nut. This type is for decorative use.

Wing nut—for use in disassembling something easily.

Cap Screw

This is designed to be installed into something that is prethreaded. It comes in various sizes based on diameter and threads per inch. For example, $\frac{1}{4} \times 20$, would mean that the bolt is $\frac{1}{4}''$ in diameter and has 20 threads to the inch. A typical (and common) application would be to secure an electrical motor to its housing.

Stud Bolt

This device has lag screw threads on one end and machine screw threads on the other, with a smooth portion in between. It is commonly used to assemble furniture: The lag screw portion is screwed into the frame of the piece, while the machine screw portion screws into a threaded socket in the leg. Hence, when the leg gets loose, you can turn the nut to tighten it.

The practical value of a stud bolt for the do-it-yourselfer is for hanging fixtures. For example, in a garage the lag screw portion could be sunk into a joist or ceiling beam, while the fixture, which has a threaded hole, is screwed onto the projecting machine screw part.

Stud bolt

Eyebolt

This is classified by shank size; the eye size is fixed. These bolts are commonly used for hanging up clothesline and are used with nuts. They come galvanized or zinc plated.

These are also considered bolts. Eyebolt is at upper left.

Stove Bolt

This bolt is used to join pieces of metal. It is slotted and is commonly used in the smaller sizes ⅛", ³⁄₁₆", and ⁵⁄₃₂". Stove bolts are often used in assembling metal shelves.

BUYING TIPS FOR BOLTS

Machine and carriage bolts will be more expensive than lag screws, so if you have a choice, use a lag screw whenever possible.

Carriage and machine bolts come in two styles: rolled and cut thread. The cut thread is better. Here, the manufacturer cuts the thread right into the steel shaft in making the bolt. In making the rolled kind, the thread is rolled onto the shaft separately. The reason is that less metal is used. In the smaller sizes it doesn't matter, but in the larger sizes a problem can occur: The shank, or smooth part of the bolt, may fit the drilled hole perfectly, but the rolled (threaded) part may not. So you drill a hole for the threads to fit—and the shank is a loose, sloppy fit.

Typical hardware for hanging a plant.

Plant Hangers

In recent years people have returned to the earth, and many who do not have some handy acreage nearby have taken to keeping their own plants at home. This has led to a boom in plant hangers, hardware used to hang the plants. Today there are a number of devices for hanging plants.

Plant holder (Edward A. Designs) has an 8-inch clear plastic platform with circular upper ring and four clear plastic tube lines. It can be adjusted in height.

Macramé

This is not as popular as it once was, but macramé hangers are still available. Basically, it is rope that is looped around the pot and hung from some piece of hardware, such as a screw eye or toggle bolt. The do-it-yourselfer can make macrame hangers, but they are available commercially. One company, Edward A. Designs, makes hangers that are thin, almost transparent, the idea being to make the hanger as unobtrusive as possible.

Wire

This may also be used to hang plants. As noted in the wire section (see page 92), there is wire that is flexible and can be easily formed to hold plants.

Hanging Track

This is relatively new. Here, a track is secured to the ceiling, and four or five plants are suspended with hooks from corresponding pieces of hardware that ride along in the track.

Plant hanger track (Stanley) comes with swivel hooks on which you attach a rope or cord and then hang the plants. Track should be screwed to joists or ceiling beams so it can support plant weight.

Shelves

Plants have been supported by shelves for years. However, the brackets used to support shelves that support planters are generally fancier than usual.

Chain

Decorative chain is another popular means of hanging plants. It comes in brass finish and colors. It can be secured to the ceiling with fancy toggle bolts or hooks that screw into wood or ceiling material. For more information, see pages 8–13.

Swivel hanger (Gries Reproducer) is a common plant hanger. It can be hooked onto just about anything. When cord or chain is attached to it, the plant can be rotated 360°, a plus if you want to face the plant toward sunlight at various times of the day.

Plant bracket mounts on the wall and then the plant is hung from it with another chain, rope, or were.

Pulleys

Another type of hardware available for hanging plants is a pulley-type arrangement that works like venetian blinds. Pulling on a cord raises or lowers the plants. On display they hang out of the way and they can be lowered for watering.

The hardware that secures wire, rope, or chain to the surface is normally sold separately from these items. As you've no doubt gathered, it would be quite easy to create your own sets of hangers based on information in this book.

The most important consideration in hanging any plant is to make sure that the hardware and the material it's hung from can support it. If you are hanging a plant on Sheetrock, you shouldn't really go above 5 pounds (plaster in good condition allows more weight). Above that weight the toggle bolt used to secure it can pull through the material. If you can turn a screw eye into a ceiling beam or joist, then you can go a lot heavier— say, 20 pounds. It should be remembered that not only the weight of the plant must be taken into account; there is also the additional weight of the water.

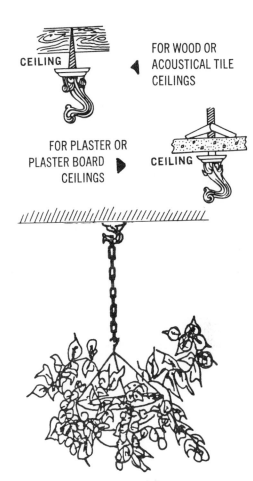

Hangers (Yorkville) above are for use as noted. Screw type works best in acoustical tile. Make sure the surface can support the plant.

Brackets such as one shown come in various fancy finishes. The one shown is embossed gold.

Rope and Cord

The main difference between rope and cord is size and, therefore, strength. In general, material that is above ⅛″ in diameter is called rope, while anything below that is cord. Of the two, rope is the more common product.

There are a number of rope types that you will commonly find in hardware stores. It's usually sold from reels by the foot.

Manila

Most common of all is manila rope, which is made from hemp and is the best natural fiber rope you can buy. It resists sunlight, it won't melt (as nylon will, for example), it won't stretch much, and it ties quite well so it will hold knots. It, like most rope, is generally available in sizes ranging from ¼″ up to ¾″.

Sisal

Sisal rope is another natural fiber rope. It has less strength than manila rope and is less durable. It should be thought of only for temporary jobs. For day-to-day tying and untying applications, manila is much better.

Nylon

There are a couple of kinds of nylon rope, each with different characteristics. The big advantage of twisted nylon, one type, is that it stretches a lot. If you have an application where you want rope to be able to take a shock—to stretch, that is—then nylon would be a good choice.

Nylon, in addition to being very strong, is also resistant to chemicals, oils, and the like. On the negative side, it has a low burning point, and the twist type will unravel when cut. To prevent this, a good trick is to hold a flame under the cut end. This will melt the nylon and fuse the loose strands into a solid nub.

The other type of nylon is solid braid. This type of nylon won't unravel when it's cut, as the twist type will.

Polypropelene

Polypropelene rope is rot and mildew resistant and also resists chemicals well. Its outstanding characteristic, however, is that it floats. As such, it makes a good rope to mark off boundaries of swimming areas. Its usual color is bright yellow, but red is sometimes available.

Clothesline

As mentioned, the major difference between cord and rope is one of size. Cord is usually less than ⅛″ in diameter, though this, as mentioned, is not absolute.

Most common cord is what is simply called clothesline cord. It comes in a number of styles. One is braided cotton. This is made with a filler inside it to give it bulk and body. It is commonly sold by the hank.

Another type of clothesline cord is plastic. This consists of a film of vinyl over a wire. Its major advantage is that it is easy to clean—a wipe with a damp cloth does it. Plastic clothesline is more expensive than cotton.

The other type of clothesline is poly clothesline. This is braided.

Cotton clothesline is usually sold by the hank.

Twine

Twine might be defined as a lightweight version of rope and cord. There are various kinds. Jute twine is designed for wrapping parcels. It has a fuzzy surface, which tends to make it stick to itself and hold well when tied. Sisal twine is also available and is very inexpensive. One other available cord is mason's line. This is a thin, strong cord that comes in balls.

Accessories

The main accessories for rope and cord are the snap, swivel-eye snap, and pulley. These are available separately in various sizes. The snap is just that: The rope or cord is tied to the eye on one end of the snap. Pulling a button on the snap opens the snap mechanism for hooking onto whatever you wish.

The swivel-eye snap is the same thing, except that it rotates 360°, preventing the line from twisting. As such, it's a popular accessory on rope used for dog runs.

The snap is one of the main accessories for rope and cord.

The swivel-eye snap is basically the same thing, except that it swivels 380°, preventing the line from twisting.

The double snap can also come in handy.

The pulley comes in various sizes, usually 5″ and 7″ diameter. It is mainly designed for use with clothesline. With enough pulleys in proper position, however, you can rig up a winch. This might come in handy for such jobs as lifting heavy home improvement materials to the second floor of a home or to the roof.

BUYING TIPS

In addition to buying it by the foot, rope, cord, and twine are available in packages designated for specific uses. For example, Lehigh Sales and Products, Inc., packages rope for tie-downs, winches, craft and macrame uses, clothesline, and so on. If hardware is required, the rope or cord will come with it.

In some cases you will find it convenient to buy the material this way, but you'll usually save money if you buy it by the foot.

Safe Working Load (SWL) refers to the maximum number of pounds of pressure or weight that should be applied to rope that is in good condition; that is, really, brand new when the rope is used where there is danger to life, limb or property. Breaking Strength (ST) is the theoretical strength of the rope in non critical situations—no danger to life, limb, or property.

Rope is commonly sold from reels.

Properties of Rope
★ ★ ★ ★ = best characteristics

	Nylon	Poly	Manila	Sisal
Shock load	★ ★ ★ ★	★ ★ ★	★ ★	★
Rot resistance	★ ★ ★ ★	★ ★ ★ ★	★	★
Mildew resistance	★ ★ ★ ★	★ ★ ★ ★	★	★
Sunlight resistance	★ ★	★	★ ★ ★ ★	★ ★ ★ ★
Handling	★ ★ ★ ★	★ ★ ★	★ ★	★
Heat	weakens at 350°	weakens at 150°	unaffected	unaffected
Storage	can store wet	can store wet	must store dry	must store dry
Oil and gas	★ ★ ★ ★	★ ★ ★ ★	★ ★	★ ★
Acid resistance	★ ★ ★	★ ★ ★ ★	★	★
Abrasion	★ ★ ★ ★	★ ★	★ ★ ★	★ ★
Durability	★ ★ ★ ★	★ ★ ★	★ ★ ★	★
Floats	no	yes	no	no

Breaking Strength of Rope
ST = breaking strength*   SWL = safe working load**

Diameter	Nylon twisted	Nylon solid braid	Poly twisted	Poly hollow braid	Manila	Sisal
	ST (SWL)	ST (SWL)	ST (SWL)	ST (SWL)	ST (SWL)	ST (SWL)
1/8″ (#4)	—	425 (85)	—	—	—	—
3/16″ (#6)	850 (75)	800 (160)	650 (75)	740 (150)	—	—
1/4″ (#8)	1,490 (124)	1,200 (240)	1,130 (113)	1,000 (200)	540 (54)	480 (96)
5/16″ (#10)	—	2,000 (400)	—	—	—	—
3/8″ (#12)	3,340 (278)	—	2,440 (244)	2,200 (440)	1,220 (122)	1,080 (216)
1/2″	5,750 (525)	—	3,780 (420)	—	2,380 (264)	2,120 (424)

*Breaking Strength (ST) is the theoretical strength of the rope in noncritical situations—no danger to life, limb or property.

**Safe Working Load (SWL) refers to the maximum number of pounds of pressure or weight that should be applied to rope that is in good condition; that is, really, brand new when the rope is used where there is danger to life, limb or property.

Screening

Screening is available in four kinds of material: aluminum, galvanized steel, bronze, and fiberglass.

Metallic screening normally comes in large rolls, from which you buy by the foot. It is available in a variety of widths: 24″, 28″, 32″, 36″, and so on up to 48″. Colors are usually bright metal or galvanized or the natural color of the metal, but gray, green, and gold are also available.

Metal screening also comes in precut rolls. For example, Phifer Wire Products sells their Brite-Kote Quik-Tak Redi-Rolls in standard lengths of 6′ and in widths from 24″ to 48″.

Fiberglass screening can also be bought from rolls or in precut pieces. It is generally gray or green.

Another type of screening that has emerged since the furor over energy is the so-called solar screening. This is designed to screen out the sun's rays—remove the heat—while allowing visibility and ventilation. Phifer's SunScreen is one such product. It is made of aluminum and fiberglass, with different wire shapes (flat and round) combining to form a weave that blocks the sun's heat and glare. Phifer says that the fiberglass blocks 75 percent of the sun's rays and lowers room temperature an average of 15 degrees. The aluminum, the company says, is less efficient.

INSTALLATION TIPS

There are a couple of tricks professional installers use that can make installing your own screening much easier.

The first is not really a trick but a tool. It is commonly called a screening tool and consists of a wood handle with a metal wheel mounted on each end; one of the wheels has a concave edge, while the other has a convex edge.

To install a piece of aluminum screening, first cut a piece an inch or two larger all around than the frame. Then use this trick: Use a pair of C-clamps to hold the screen to one of the edges. As you work on the screen, these clamps will prevent the material from moving out of position, a common problem. If you don't have C-clamps (or some other holding device) around, you can buy little ones (2″ high) cheaply.

Pull the screen flat to the opposite edge and use the convex wheel to gently push the screening down until it bottoms into the groove. Then take a piece of spline (the rubbery material used to hold the screen edges in grooves around the frame) and use the concave wheel to work it (use short strokes) into the groove on the screen. From this point on you don't need the clamps. Remove them and secure the screening to the opposite side of the frame. Secure the remaining two sides. There's no

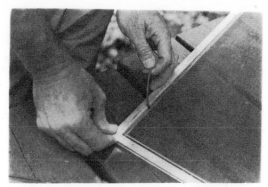

The first step in replacing screen is to remove spline, the flexible material that wedges the edge of the screening into the groove. A screwdriver tip helps.

Once you can grab the end you can pull the spline out in one piece.

Cut a new piece of screening slightly larger than the frame, then place it over the frame and secure one side with C-clamps. Here the author improvised with one clamp and a pair of locking pliers.

Working on the side opposite the one secured, use a convex wheel on a screening tool to push the screen edge into the groove. There's no need to pull the screen taut as you do this—just flatten it.

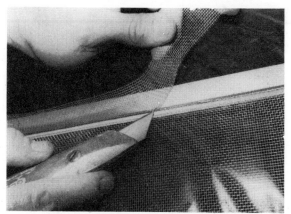

Use a utility knife to trim away excess screening, using the frame as a guide for the blade, and the job's done.

Soak a piece of spline in warm soapy water. Then cut it about an inch shorter than the groove (it will stretch as you place it), and set it in the groove. (Use the concave wheel to push it into the groove.) Try to do this in one "roll," not in short strokes. When this side is done, insert the spline on the opposite side and then the other sides. Clamps aren't needed on last three sides.

need to pull the screen taut. Just keep it smooth and flat and will pull taut as you work.

Use a sharp single-edge razor blade or utility knife (preferably) to trim the screen as you go. Blades should be changed frequently.

It is usually possible to use the old spline to secure the new screen. Just wash and soak it in warm soapy water to make it pliable. You can also buy new spline in small packages. It is best to take a piece of the old material with you so that the dealer can give you the correct size. Spline comes in five or six different diameters.

Screw Eyes and Screw Hooks

Screw eyes and screw hooks are handy devices used for a variety of purposes, such as hanging things and hooking things together.

Screw eyes come in a variety of wire gauges and lengths. The eyes are classified by number depending on size. As the eye gets larger, the number gets smaller. So, for example, a no. 9 screw eye might have an inside diameter of ½", while a no. 000 would have one twice that size.

Screw eyes

Also, as the eye gets bigger, the length of the device gets longer and the wire diameter thicker. Screw eyes (and screw hooks) vary in size from tiny ones ½" long to large ones 3" long.

You don't need to know the number system to get the size you need. An examination of what's available and a knowledge of the job you have to do will tell you quickly which size you need.

Screw hooks are commonly used for hanging things from ceilings, where they are screwed into wood members, but they can be used anywhere you need them as long as the threads bite into the material and hold securely.

A variation on the regular screw hook is the square bend hook. Here, instead of a rounded hook, the hook part is formed in an L shape. It is installed so that the L is horizontal. It supports such things as drapery rods.

If you use a screw eye and screw hook together, the sizes must be the same. A no. 9 screw hook goes with a no. 9 screw eye, and so on. In some cases the items will be carded together; in others they are bought loose.

There are a number of devices that are basically combinations of screw hooks and eyes.

Gate Hook

The gate hook is one such combination. There is a screw eye that screws into the gate or post, while a corresponding hook (on gate or post) goes into the eye. These sizes must be matched, but this is not a problem because all necessary hardware comes in one package. Gate hook and eyes commonly come in lengths of from 1″ to 5″, but you can get them all the way up to 18″ long.

Screw hook. These also come in many different sizes.

Square bend hook

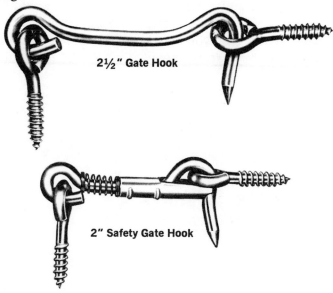

2½″ Gate Hook

2″ Safety Gate Hook

Cup Hook

This is a rounded screw hook with a plate or shoulder, the main purpose of which is to prevent the device from being driven too far into the wood. Cup hooks are designed for hanging cups under cabinet shelves. They vary in size from ½″

Cup hooks, round, and shoulder types

to 1¼" and are almost always brass, since they have a decorative function.

A variation on the rounded cup hook is the shoulder hook, an L-shaped screw hook with a shoulder. These also are available in sizes up to 2".

An easy way to install a cup hook in soft wood is simply to push it in place.

Clothesline Hook

This looks like an enlarged cup hook except that it has a plate with holes to accept screws. It enables you to mount it securely with small screws that do not bite too deeply; in other words, you don't have to run a big screw hook into a material (say, siding) and risk damaging it or not be able to get a secure grip because the material is too thin.

Hammock Hook

This is a variation on the clothesline hook; two types are common. One has a plate with screw holes in it, the other is simply a hefty screw-and-eye affair. Which one you would use would depend on where the hammock is being mounted, but the different types give you a wider choice of mounting locations because they can be mounted where the material is thick or thin.

There are also hooks and eyes with plates available for TV cable. Here the plate handily hides the hole made for the cable.

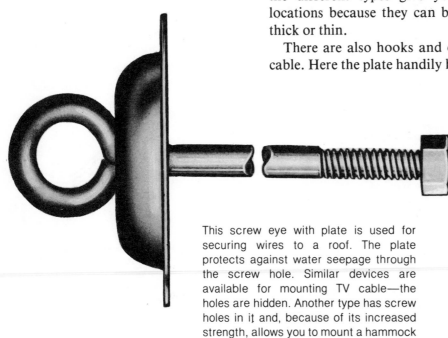

This screw eye with plate is used for securing wires to a roof. The plate protects against water seepage through the screw hole. Similar devices are available for mounting TV cable—the holes are hidden. Another type has screw holes in it and, because of its increased strength, allows you to mount a hammock in thin material (you don't need a big screw eye).

Flat Hook and Eye

If you have need of a hook and eye that lies flat, there are brass hooks and eyes (Charles O. Larson has hooks that range from ¾" to 2½" with corresponding eyes). Here the hook is squared off and lies flat. You can use the device with an eye of the proper size or simply run a wood screw into the box and hook the hook on that. Such devices are often used to secure chest or cabinet lids.

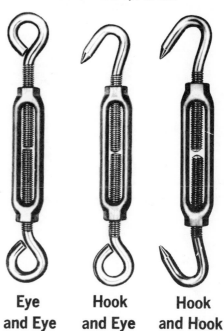

Brass hook and eye lie flat.

Turnbuckles

The turnbuckle is used when you want to brace something. The body of the device is basically a barrel with two threaded rods sticking out of it—one left-handed thread, the other right-handed. When cable or rod is attached and the barrel turned, the rod or cable is tightened or loosened.

Turnbuckles come in three forms. The barrel may have an eye at each end, a hook at one end and an eye at the other, or a hook at each end. Thus, you have flexibility for attaching cable, rod, rope, and other items. For example, on the eye of a turnbuckle you might have a snap fastener and rope, on the other end a cable attached to a hook.

Eye and Eye　　**Hook and Eye**　　**Hook and Hook**

Turnbuckles

Turnbuckle for taking sag from screen doors come with rods attached

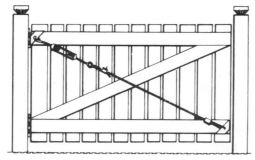

Turnbuckle and rod may also be used to take sag from gates

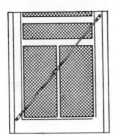

Turnbuckle in action

Commonly, turnbuckles come zinc plated, but you can buy galvanized ones in large sizes. Indeed, you can get them up to 2' long.

One particularly useful turnbuckle is used for screen doors. The turnbuckle and rod is available in one package and is normally 42" long. By attaching it to the diagonal corners of a screen door you can straighten out any warpage or sag.

Screws

Screws are on a par with nails in terms of usefulness to the do-it-yourselfer. They are stronger than nails and have the advantage of being able to be taken out when desired; you can disassemble the job at will.

There are four things to consider when selecting a screw for the job: finish, length, weight or gauge, and head.

Screws can be plain steel, blued and dipped—which means they're partially weather resistant to moisture—galvanized, brass, or chrome plated.

Screws range in size up to about 4"; when you get beyond 4", consider using a lag bolt; you'll have difficulty turning a very long screw (a lag bolt is turned with a wrench). The length you use will depend on the thickness of the material you're using. The screw should be about ¼" to ½" shorter than the total thickness of the material you're driving it into.

Screws are also classified according to the diameter or gauge, commonly ranging from no. 5 to no. 14, though larger sizes are available. The gauge refers to the diameter under the head. Since the screw tapers, the gauge gets smaller as the screw gets thinner. Screws of the same gauge are available in different lengths. Screw sizes are always given in terms of length and gauge: ½" × no. 8, for example.

There are three types of head: flat, round, and oval.

Flathead Screws

Flathead screw

These have a countersunk head, meaning that they are tapered to be recessed or sunk flush into the wood. To do this, you first drill a pilot hole that is as thick as the threaded part would be without the threads. (The table on page 71 gives drill bit sizes to use.) A good tool for countersinking is Stanley's

Screwmate. Indeed, this can both countersink and counterbore (set the head of the screw below the surface).

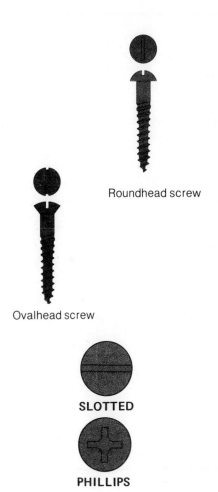

Roundhead screw

Ovalhead screw

SLOTTED

PHILLIPS

Roundhead Screws

These are easier screws to turn down tight. For greater holding power you can put washers under them. Since their heads are meant to be left exposed, roundhead screws are often used in utility work where appearance is not a concern.

Ovalhead Screws

The heads of these screws are partially recessed. They are decorative screws and, as such, normally come with a brass or chrome-plated finish.

Straight Slot and Phillips Screws

Head styles may also vary in another way: the turning design. There are many different kinds, but the most popular are the straight slot and the Phillips. The slotted head screw has just that—a slot across the head of the screw. The Phillips head has crisscross slots and is turned with a Phillips screwdriver. The latter is supposed to allow more turning power to be applied, but in home application this isn't a factor. The straight slot is fine.

Machine Screws

These screws are completely threaded and have flat ends and heads that may be either round or flat. They come in non-corrosive materials, such as brass or chrome plated, and also plain steel. Machine screws, so called because their original use was in metal machinery parts, are generally used with items that are threaded. For example, they are commonly used with hollow wall anchors (Mollies).

They come in various gauges—nos. 4, 6, 8, 10, 12—and the larger the gauge, the heavier the diameter. Above no. 12 the diameters are ¼", but smaller sizes are more commonly available.

Machine screws are also characterized by the number of threads per inch. They may have either 24 or 32 threads to the

Machine screw

inch. The former is called the National Coarse Thread, the latter National Fine Thread. Taps and dies are available for making threads in various gauges as well. Screws are designated by gauge and threads. For example a 10-32 screw means one that has a no. 10 gauge and 32 threads to the inch. An 8-24 would mean a no. 8 screw with 24 threads to the inch. The finer the thread a screw has, the better it will grip.

Machine screws come in lengths of from ½" to 4". They are not very strong screws and are generally used in fastening lightweight materials. If you are fastening something like thin-gauge sheet metal, the screws should be used with washers and nuts. Machine screws come carded and by the box.

Sheet metal screw with panhead.

Sheet Metal Screws

These differ from wood screws in a number of ways but chiefly in that there is no smooth shank part: The screw is threaded all the way from the tip to under the head.

Sheet metal screws are designed to drill their own thread. They are for use in thin-gauge sheet metal, such as holding parts on aluminum storm doors.

Head styles vary, but the panhead with the single slot is the most popular and will be adequate for most purposes.

Pilot Holes

Pilot holes should be drilled for all screws driven into hardwood. Otherwise, you will have great difficulty driving them, and the wood may be split. In softwood, such as pine, pilot holes are not required.

If you are driving screws into hardwood, the pilot hole in the first piece of wood should be bored so it freely accommodates the screw shank (see *B* in the drawing). The hole should be slightly smaller than the shank in the second piece of wood, as shown in the chart below. Also, the hole depth in the second piece of wood should be about one-half the screw's length, with the screw at least ⅛" shorter than the combined thicknesses of the two pieces of wood. This job can be greatly simplified by using one of the commercially available countersinking devices, such as Stanley's Screwmate.

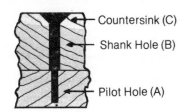

Countersink (C)

Shank Hole (B)

Pilot Hole (A)

| Screw size | Pilot hole (A) | | | | Shank clearance holes (B) | | Countersink (C) |
| | Hardwoods | | Softwoods | | | | |
	Twist bit (Nearest size in fractions of an inch)	Drill gauge no. To be used for maximum holding power	Twist bit (Nearest size in fractions of an inch)	Drill gauge no. To be used for maximum holding power	Twist bit (Nearest size in fractions of an inch)	Drill gauge no. or letter To be used for maximum holding power	Number of auger bit To be counter-bore for sinking head (by 16ths)
2	—	54	1/32	65	3/32	42	3
3	1/16	53	3/64	58	7/64	37	4
4	1/16	51	3/64	55	7/64	32	4
5	5/64	47	1/16	53	1/8	30	4
6	—	44	1/16	52	9/64	27	5
7	—	39	1/16	51	5/32	22	5
8	7/64	35	5/64	48	11/64	18	6
9	7/64	33	5/64	45	3/16	14	6
10	1/8	31	3/32	43	3/16	10	6
11	—	29	3/32	40	13/64	4	7
12	—	25	7/64	38	7/32	2	7
14	3/16	14	7/64	32	1/4	D	8
16	—	10	9/64	29	17/64	I	9
18	13/64	6	9/64	26	19/64	N	10
20	7/32	3	11/64	19	21/64	P	11
24	1/4	D	3/16	15	3/8	V	12

Shelf Supports

There are three common kinds of supporting hardware for shelves: utility brackets, standards and brackets, and pilasters. One other way is with special metal or plastic clips called simply shelf supports.

Utility Brackets

These brackets are mounted directly on the wall with screws, preferably into studs (if the studs don't fall in the proper places—studs are normally 16″ apart, 24″ in older homes—you can use hollow wall anchors). The shelves of your choice are then laid across the brackets.

Utility brackets are, as the name implies, for utility. There is nothing particularly fancy or decorative about them, though they do come in various colors such as gold and black.

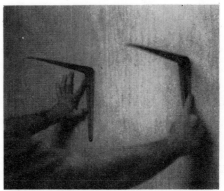

Utility bracket. It has holes in both legs in order to fasten it to the wall and secure the shelves.

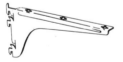

Fancy utility bracket can be used as shown, supporting arm up or down

Note hooked end of shelf bracket.

Standards and Brackets

This type of hardware allows flexibility of use. You can move the shelves to varying heights for accommodating taller or shorter items as the need arises.

Standards are vertically slotted pieces of metal that are secured to studs or wall material. They have predrilled holes for receiving screws, which are usually 6″ to 8″ apart. The bracket has a hook-shaped part on it that latches into the slots on the standards, and shelves are then laid across the brackets. Hence, if you want to move the shelves, you simply unhook the brackets and relocate them in new slots.

Standards and brackets come in various finishes and are more expensive than utility brackets. Sizes (the top part of the bracket the shelf rests on) normally run from 4″ to 18″ in increments of 2″.

If you are just supporting books, rather than heavy hi-fi equipment, a TV, or the like, you can use hollow wall anchors to mount the standards. But if the weight you wish to support is too heavy, you run the risk of the anchor pulling out of the wall material.

Sometimes the standards and brackets from different companies are interchangeable, but in most instances you must use the same brand.

Pilasters

These are mounted inside kitchen or other cabinets because they're not made to be attractive. There are standards, but instead of the slots being vertical, they are horizontal in order to accept small clips. Pilasters may be adjusted to some degree.

BUYING TIPS

Pilasters usually are made of steel, but they may be aluminum. There is no particular advantage of one over the other, except that if you need maximum strength, steel is better.

Shelf Supports

Shelf supports may be either plastic or metal. They are mounted in ¼″ holes made in cabinets; when the shelves are laid across them, the supports are locked firmly in place by the weight.

Standards and brackets installed

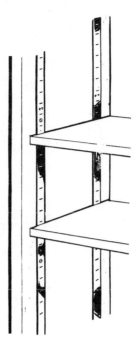

Pilasters are used inside cabinets but may also be used outside.

Close-up view of pilaster

Shelf supports. These may be either plastic or metal. The round part fits into a predrilled hole. The weight on the support locks it into place.

Mounting these supports is not easy, simply because drilling a series of holes in line with one another is not easy. It is best to make a template for drilling them.

Springs

There are three kinds of springs for home use: extension, compression, and torsion. The first two types are widely used, whereas the torsion spring is less common.

Springs come in various wire gauges and lengths; indeed, there are hundreds of sizes available. Most are zinc plated to resist corrosion and rust, so they may be used outside. Ones that are painted with black enamel are also available; these can be used indoors only. Springs that are chrome plated are also available, though not commonly.

Extension Spring

This type of spring consists, like the compression spring, of wire in a coil shape. The ends may have either a closed loop or a hook or a variation on this theme. The variations lend flexibility of use: You can either hook the spring into something or vice versa—hook something onto the spring.

The more coils an extension spring has—and depending on the wire gauge—the longer it will expand.

One special extension spring worth noting has extra-long—3″ or so—hooks on the ends. This type is useful getting into tight places, such as an oven door. Instead of having to snake your hand in and attach a spring with a short hook, you can fish the long hook in until it can grab on.

Another special spring is one used on screen doors. The end of this spring has a cap with a threaded eyebolt and nut. By rotating the bolt you can draw up or relax the tension in order to make the door close either quickly or slowly, as you wish.

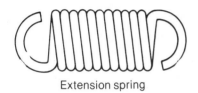

Extension spring

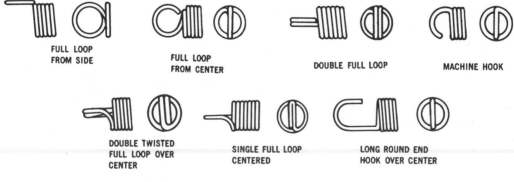

FULL LOOP FROM SIDE

FULL LOOP FROM CENTER

DOUBLE FULL LOOP

MACHINE HOOK

DOUBLE TWISTED FULL LOOP OVER CENTER

SINGLE FULL LOOP CENTERED

LONG ROUND END HOOK OVER CENTER

Extension springs come with ends in various shapes that increase their versatility.

Compression Spring

This type of spring is used when you want to push two things apart, such as shafts and wheels on toys. It is primarily a replacement spring.

Again, wire gauge and the length of the spring determines how much compression the spring exerts. Unlike the extension spring, the compression type does not have hooks or loops at the ends. Ends are either squared off or plain. In the first case the end of the spring does not project at all, but is flat; in the second, the spring projects a bit. The squared-off end is useful if you need a spring that will lie flat between things.

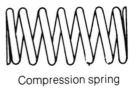

Compression spring

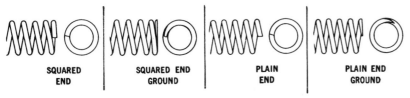

| SQUARED END | SQUARED END GROUND | PLAIN END | PLAIN END GROUND |

Compression spring ends

Torsion Spring

This type of spring is rarely used. Its main use is on doors, where it is slipped over the top of the hinge pin and gives the door a spring-door closing action that it did not have before.

BUYING TIP

Because there are hundreds of springs available, the fastest way to get the one you want is to bring the old one into the store. Most hardware stores have a board on which a variety of springs are displayed, and it will be a simple matter to match up your old one with one of them. The idea, of course, is to get one with the same tension and ends.

Springs may be bought loose or carded, and in assortments. Ajax Wire Speciality Co., Inc., for example, sells a U-Fix-It assortment of compression, extension, and torsion types—seventy-five springs in all. However, before you invest in such a purchase, you should carefully evaluate your need for springs, for you may never use most of them.

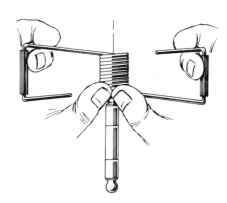

Torsion spring. This is fitted over a door hinge to give it spring tension.

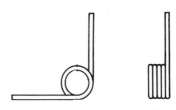

Two views of torsion spring

Storm Door, Patio Door, and Garage Door Hardware

Over the last few years the American public has been repeatedly reminded of the virtues of storm doors. They provide a line of defense against bad weather: Cold air and drafts have more difficulty getting into the house, while heat has more difficulty getting out. In the summer, glass or Plexiglas panels that clip into the frame may be removed and replaced with screening if desired.

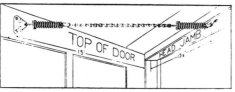

A typical storm door closer. It has an adjusting mechanism so the door can be opened and closed at the desired speed.

Storm doors should also have a spring attached so the door cannot open too wide and pull the other parts (such as the closer) out of the door.

Storm Door Hardware

The main parts of a storm door are the lock mechanism and the pneumatic cylinder, which can be adjusted to close slowly so that the door will not slam but fast enough to ensure that it will latch. There is also an extension spring between the frame and the door so that the door can only open to a certain distance; otherwise the hinges would have to take too much stress and could be damaged.

Like window hardware, it is best to remove the part that you want to replace in order to ensure getting the proper size and style; there are quite a few variations, and the screw holes must be in the same places on the replacement piece that they are on the existing door.

Lock mechanisms. Many lock mechanisms on storm doors do not lock, but there is one type that will let you lock the door with the flip of a lever or button. This is handy when you want to open the interior door to let lots of light in but want some measure of security, perhaps just enough to keep your pet from getting outside.

If you want more security when you leave home, you can also get lock mechanisms with key cylinders. Again, make sure the screw holes match. If you have a wooden storm door, a good match is also necessary.

Storm door closers. Most closers are of the "bicycle pump" variety, that is, the adjustment on them is somewhat cantankerous, but you can usually get them set so that the door closes and latches but does not slam too hard.

There are other door closers made for all kinds and sizes of doors that have better adjusting and closing mechanisms, such as the large ones found on the doors of public buildings. You might look for one of these if you have a particularly difficult problem with your door (such as the wind always catching it). The closer should be matched to the size and weight of your door.

Patio Door Hardware

Here, too, parts must match. You should not attempt to interchange parts, even if it seems that you can. For example, on wheels that appear to be the same size there might be a slight difference in thickness, and even though the wheels "fit," you won't get the same fast rolling action as you would if you used a proper size part. The manufacturer's name will often be stamped on the unit, usually on the track. This can be an aid in obtaining parts.

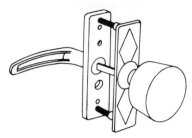

Lock for a storm door. This does not have a locking feature from the outside, but looks can be bought this way. The key in buying storm, patio, and garage door hardware is to take the part to the dealer so he can match it with a replacement.

Garage Door Hardware

Hardware for garage doors also varies considerably. Several of these parts are shown in the illustrations. It is suggested that here, too, you remove the part and bring it to your local hardware store dealer for replacement.

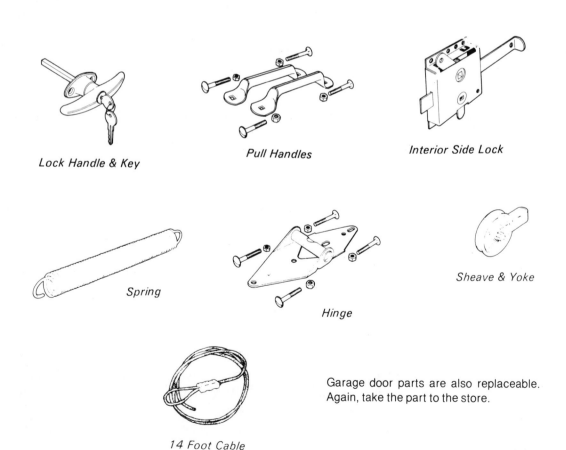

Lock Handle & Key

Pull Handles

Interior Side Lock

Spring

Hinge

Sheave & Yoke

14 Foot Cable

Garage door parts are also replaceable. Again, take the part to the store.

Threaded Rod

Threaded rod is a metal rod that is threaded from one end to the other. With appropriate washers and nuts it can be used for a variety of jobs—hanging, fastening, mounting, bracing, or supporting things. In some situations, bolts are not suitable because of limited thread portions (for example a 6″ bolt may only have 1″ or 1½″ of thread); threaded rod can serve well here.

Threaded rod is usually made of steel and can be cold bent (no heat required), which increases its usefulness.

The rod comes in a variety of lengths and diameters. Commonly hardware stores and the like will carry it in lengths of 2′ and 3′. Diameters are commonly 3/16″, ¼″, 5/16″, 3/8″, and ½″. However, it may be had in ten or twelve diameters all the way up to 1¼″ and in lengths of 6′, 10′, and 12′. To obtain these sizes, you may have to place a special order or visit a number of hardware stores. The rod may be had with either a plain steel or blue bright electroplate finish. The ends are usually color coded according to sizes.

Threaded rod may be cut with a hacksaw or a bolt cutter. Since the threads run along the rod at a slight angle, it is easy to create burrs on the cut ends that will make running nuts on the rod difficult or impossible. For this reason, when cutting rod it is suggested that you follow this procedure:

1. Run a nut down from each end of the rod until they are almost touching and flanking the line where you will cut.

2. Cut the rod.

3. Run the nuts off the rod from the cut ends. Since the metal is relatively soft, this will dress the ends, in effect reshaping threads properly.

Precut Rod

Threaded steel rods of various lengths, diameters, and shapes are also available in shaped pieces such as U-bolts and eyebolts (one company who makes them is Medalist Redi-Bolt). The cards they come on give hints on their use. They are zinc plated, making them okay for outside use.

Stainless Steel Rod

While few handymen would have use for threaded stainless steel rod, the material is available. Star Stainless Screw Company carries stock sizes of 2′, 3′, and 6′ in various diameters. The company also makes it in various shapes, such as U-bolts and J-bolts. You will likely have to get it on special order from a hardware store.

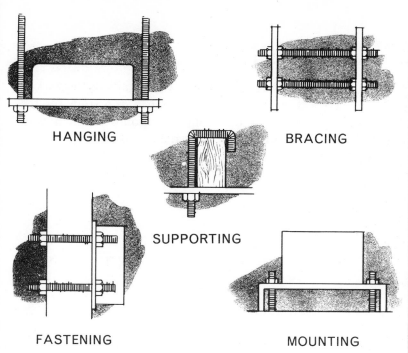

HANGING

BRACING

SUPPORTING

FASTENING

MOUNTING

There are various uses for threaded rod.

Turn the nuts off the cut ends. This takes out burrs and re-forms threads.

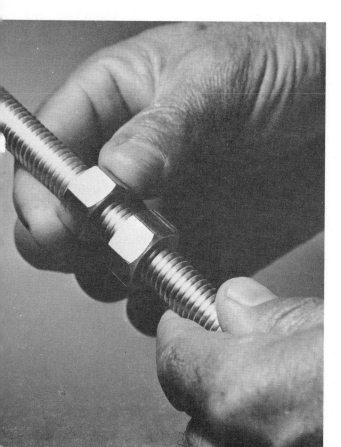

This fine series of pictures supplied by Bethlehem Steel shows how to cut rod. First, slip the nuts down to a point flanking the cut line.

Cut with a hacksaw.

79

installation

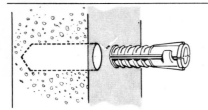

Hole is drilled into concrete for sleeve of expansion shield

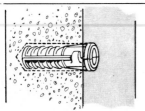

Expansion shield is placed in hole

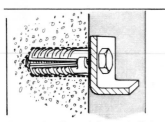

Screw is slipped through fixture, then into sleeve and tightened, expanding sleeve and locking fastener in place

If points on hollow wall anchor don't grip wall the fastener will turn round and round when screw is turned. To hold fastener stationary hardware stores have a tiny tool that's free.

Wall Fasteners

Wall fasteners are useful where screws or nails can't work—that is, where's there no solid surface, such as a stud, for the nail or screw to bite into. While commonly called a wall fastener, these devices can also be used on ceilings.

At first glance there is a bewildering array of fasteners, but it can be reduced to three basic kinds.

Expansion Shields for Masonry

The expansion shield is for hanging things on masonry surfaces. It is used like the other two kinds of fasteners discussed here. It consists of a sleeve and a screw. To use it, a hole is first drilled in the masonry that is the diameter of the sleeve, which may be lead, fiber, or plastic. The sleeve is then slipped into the hole. A screw—you'd get either a lag screw or wood screw, depending on what you're hanging—is then slipped or driven through a hole in the item to be fastened and into the sleeve and then tightened. As it is, it cuts its own thread, expanding the sleeve and locking it into the wall.

It should be noted that the size screw used should be long enough to be able to pass through the item to be hung and penetrate ¼″ beyond the end of the sleeve.

An exception to this screw-in type of installation is the kind of device that is hammered into place. One such device is the Tampin (Star). Here a machine screw is used. A hole the diameter of a prethreaded sleeve with a lead section on the bottom is drilled. The sleeve is slipped into the hole, then the machine screw is slipped through a hole in the item to be fastened and screwed down in the sleeve. The head is whacked with a special setting tool, and the lead mushrooms, locking the sleeve into place.

This type of fastener is good if you are hanging something that is threaded to accept a machine screw; the lag or wood screw, of course, wouldn't work.

Expansion shields are available in a wide variety of sizes. The bigger the device, the heavier the weight it will support.

Toggle Bolts for Hollow Wall Construction

If you want to hang something on hollow wall construction, chiefly plasterboard (Sheetrock) but also wood and plaster where there is space inside the wall, a toggle bolt may be used.

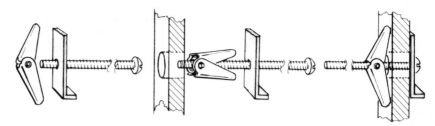

A toggle bolt is used like a hollow wall anchor. A hole is drilled, a screw is slipped through the item, then the wings on the toggle are slipped through the hole. As the screw tightens it draws the wings against the back side of the wall for a tight grip.

There are two kinds of toggle bolts. Each consists of a machine screw with collapsible "wings" threaded on it. On one the wings are spring loaded; when squeezed together and released they open; on the other type the wings are not spring-loaded (these are cheaper).

To use a spring-loaded toggle bolt, a hole is drilled in the wall that is large enough so that the toggle bolt, with its wings folded back, can be passed through. The wings are removed from the screw, the screw slipped through the item to be hung, and the wings screwed back on. The wings are folded back and the fastener slipped through the hole in the wall. Inside the wall they pop open. The screw is run down by hand, then tightened with a screwdriver. As it is, the wings grip the backside of the wall (or ceiling or floor surface). The tighter you make the screw, the harder the wings grip the wall.

The procedure is the same for toggle bolts without spring-loaded wings, except you extend the wings horizontally and slip them through the hole; inside the wall gravity flips them vertical.

It is important to remember to pass the screw through the item before slipping the toggle into the wall. Once the wings are inside, you can't back out the screw without the wings dropping off inside the wall; the fastener becomes useless.

On toggle bolts make sure that the wall cavity is deep enough to accept the toggle bolt. Toggle bolts come in very long sizes; if one is too long, the end of the screw will jam up against the back side of the other wall before you can run the screw all the way down.

There is a limit, also, on how much weight you should put on a toggle bolt. If you are hanging something from a plaster or plasterboard wall, around 50 pounds per toggle would be about right. But if you are hanging something from a plaster or plasterboard ceiling, each toggle will hold only about 5 pounds. Otherwise, the weight of the item could pull the fastener through the material. Here you should use wood screws sunk in studs.

Hollow Wall Anchors

A toggle bolt is for one-time use. A fastener that can be used and reused but is also for hollow wall construction is the hollow wall anchor, commonly called a Molly, though this is the brand name of one manufacturer, the USM Company.

This fastener has its wings built on; it comes with a machine screw. To install the fastener, first drill a hole in the wall, slip the fastener through the hole and tap it with a hammer, then tighten the screw. As the screw is tightened, the wings expand and eventually grip the back side of the wall. The screw is then removed, slipped through the item to be hung, and screwed back into the threaded sleeve in the wall. Thus, if you want to remove the item and replace it with another item, all you need to do is take out the screw.

Hollow wall anchors come in various sizes, which are based on the diameter of the machine screw used. The heavier the item, the larger the fastener must be.

When installing hollow wall anchors, there is an important thing to remember. The hole drilled in the wall must be clean and the same diameter as the fastener. Otherwise the little prongs under the head may not be able to bite into the wall tightly when you tap it with a hammer; as you turn the screw, the fastener will go around and around—it has no solid material to grip—and the wings won't expand. Use the drill bit size recommended by the manufacturer. If the fastener still goes round and round, there is a tiny tool you can get free at the hardware store to hold it stationary.

Also, the size of the flange (the smooth area just below the head) must be equal in depth to the wall thickness—if the wall is ½″ thick for example, the flange must be ½″ deep. If it isn't, the fastener will not be able to grip the surface properly.

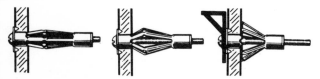

Hollow wall anchor is installed through the drilled hole of the same diameter, then tapped with a hammer so the prongs under the head can grip the surface of the wall material. A screwdriver is then used to turn the screw. As the screw turns the "wings" on the fastener, they expand until they grip the wall. The screw is then backed out, slipped through a hole in the item to be hung and reinstalled.

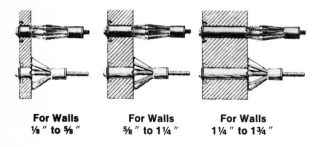

For Walls
⅛″ to ⅝″

For Walls
⅝″ to 1¼″

For Walls
1¼″ to 1¾″

Hollow wall fasteners are available for insertion in wall materials of various thicknesses. The shank on the fastener should be equal in thickness to the wall material, and the screw used should be ¼″ longer than the fastener in the installed position; that is, the thickness of the item plus that of the wall plus the thickness or length of the anchor.

Other Hollow Wall Anchors

There are a few other types of hollow wall anchors made for light applications. One is just like a Molly except that the tip is pointed; this is hammered into place; no drilled hole is required.

Another is a plastic wall anchor. This also requires that a hole be drilled. It can be used on any kind of hollow wall construction. These are for very light items, such as drapery hardware, or suspended ceiling grids.

Finally, there are jack nuts. These are simply small hollow wall anchors. They are for installing things on hollow-core doors; that is, ones where the door construction consists of a sandwich of thin wood containing a filler such as corrugated cardboard. The fasteners are not designed for solid wood doors. Here wood screws should be used.

Weather Stripping

For sealing around doors and windows there are various kinds of weather stripping one can use. Here we are concerned only with weather stripping that can be considered permanent. Caulking, tape, and the like do not fall into the hardware category and so are not considered here.

Spring Bronze

This consists of bronze strips activated by springs. It is nailed around the frame of a wood door and seals tightly when the door is closed. It is difficult to install, since it involves planing down the door so that it can fit in place.

Steel-Interlocking Weather Stripping

This consists of two parts. One part is installed on the door, the other on the frame. When the door is closed, the sections form a framework that seals the door and helps protect it from entry by burglars. It is very difficult to install properly.

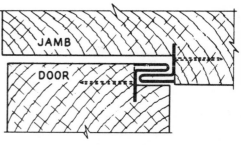

Steel interlocking weather stripping

Serrated Metal/Felt Weather Stripping

This is felt encased in metal. It is secured over gaps around windows and doors with many small nails. To make the job easier, you can use a brad driver.

This type of material doesn't look very good, but it will last and is simple to install.

Tubular Vinyl Gasket

This material has a lip that is nailed to the door or window frame. It can be used for sealing or to replace factory weather stripping on windows.

Tubular vinyl gasket shown in cross section

Vinyl stripping slips easily into place on a factory window but is difficult to install on regular windows (many nails are required).

Vinyl Channel

This is for metal-casement windows. It consists of strips of U-shaped vinyl that slip onto the edges of the window. The window must be free of distortion, or it won't work.

Aluminum-Vinyl Door Bottom

This is for sealing the gap beneath a door. Here the aluminum section is screwed to the door and mates with the vinyl section, which is attached to the floor. This hardware will last a long time.

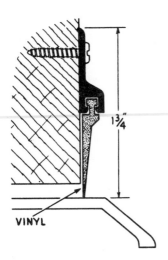

Aluminum-vinyl door bottom

Aluminum Saddle with Vinyl Gasket

Here the saddle is installed on the floor, the vinyl part on door. When closed, the vinyl seals between the door and the saddle. The door must be planed exactly so that the parts mate.

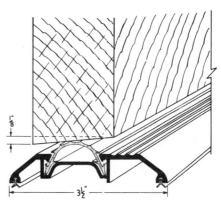

Aluminum saddle with vinyl gasket

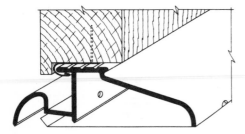

Aluminum saddle with interlocking door bottom

Aluminum Saddle with Interlocking Door Bottom

The interlock is installed on the bottom of the door. It's easier to put in than the aluminum with gasket, but the interlock can catch on rugs when the door is moved.

Aluminum and Vinyl Strips

These are strips of aluminum with vinyl facing. They are installed on doorstops and contact the door when it is closed. They are easy to install but expensive.

Rubber Garage Door Stripping

This is nailed to the bottom of a garage door to seal the gap between it and the floor. It not only seals the door but helps reduce shock when the door is closed. It is a molded double-lip strip and gets nailed in place.

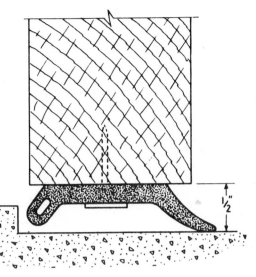

Garage door stripping

Window Hardware

There is a tremendous variety of window hardware available today. (Indeed, one company that specializes in window and door hardware, the Blaine Window Hardware Company, literally stocks thousands of different parts.) Nonetheless, the range of window hardware can be broken down to manageable proportions, namely, hardware for wood- and metal-casement windows and hardware for double-hung windows.

Casement Hardware

The reason why the hardware varies so much is, of course, because window installation construction varies and also because down through the years companies have made windows with their own peculiarities and then the companies have gone out of business. When replacing a part, then, you must normally get a particular part rather than one that can be installed in any window.

Following are parts that can be replaced on a casement window:

Casement operator or roto handle. This is the device you turn to open or close the window. Here, as with all of these parts, it is best to remove the assembly. This is done simply by unscrewing it. Then carry it down to a hardware store and match it to the replacement.

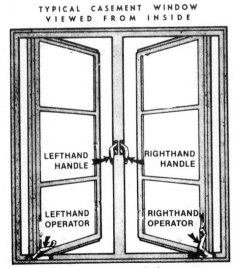

TYPICAL CASEMENT WINDOW
VIEWED FROM INSIDE

LEFTHAND HANDLE RIGHTHAND HANDLE

LEFTHAND OPERATOR RIGHTHAND OPERATOR

Casement window

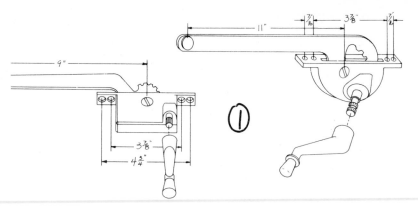

Casement operators

If the part was welded on and has broken off, it may be possible to replace it with sheet metal screws, or you can weld it back on, or, if just part of a piece broke off, you'll have to either unscrew the rest of it or break the weld.

There are a limited number of manufacturers who make these operators, perhaps two or three, and each of these makes two or three different operators. (In the trade these manufacturers are called OEM's—original equipment manufacturers. They will make windows, complete with all parts for, say, the Andersen Corporation. The manufacturer then has the parts available for selling to jobbers, who in turn sell to the hardware store.)

If the part is not available from stock (a well-stocked hardware store is your best bet), the dealer may be able to get it for you. He will commonly be visited by a jobber who specializes in, say, window parts. If you leave the operator with the dealer, he can show it to the jobber, who might have it in his stock.

If the specialized jobber doesn't have it, then you may be able to get it from the Blaine Company. They will sell you their catalogue (which normally retails for $1), for $.75 if you mention this book. The catalogue contains hundreds of drawings of various parts, and you can match up the part to what they have; or, to be absolutely sure you get the right part, ship it directly to them for replacement. They will only accept orders of more than $20. While this may seem excessive, it is reasonable when you think in terms of saving the cost of an entire new window because of the lack of one part.

Locking handle. The device used to lock a casement window is called a locking handle. The handle is lifted up, the window closed, and the handle or catch engages the keeper, which is mounted onto the window frame.

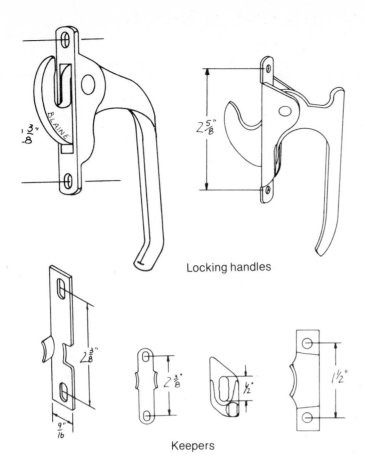

Locking handles

Keepers

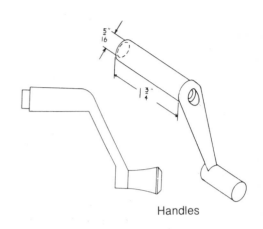

Handles

Here again your luck in being able to find a replacement for the handle or catch will depend on the particular one that's now on the window. Follow the method suggested above for obtaining the part.

One other part on a casement window is the adjustable arm between window and frame. This normally doesn't wear out.

Double-Hung Window Hardware

The locking mechanism for a double-hung wood window consists of the catch and a mechanism, called a sash lock, that swivels on the window to engage the catch. The lock is mounted on top of the inside sash and the catch on the bottom of the outside one. Here again there are many different styles, and you should follow the procedure described above for getting the casement parts.

The locking mechanism on a double-hung window is not just for security; it should also bring the window frame pieces into snug contact with each other so that the window properly seals against cold and drafts.

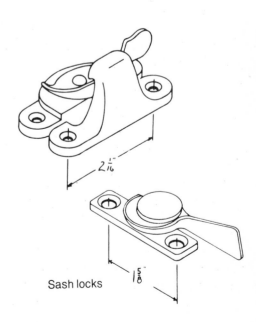

Sash locks

To do this, install the catch first, then the latch, locating each part so that when you turn the latch, there is some tension as it engages the keeper. This tension means that you are drawing the window parts together snugly. In some cases you will be able to use the old screw holes. In others you will have to make new holes, filling the old ones with Plastic Wood or a comparable product.

If you are saddled with old double-hung windows that use sash cords and counterbalance weights, you may have difficulty opening and closing windows. Or you may want to forestall difficulty by replacing the parts. There are two kinds of hardware that can help greatly. One is the tape balance, which is installed inside the cavity where the weight rides. The other are channels that can be installed within the existing frame and that accept the existing window sash.

Tape balance. The tape balance is like a long steel tape, one end of which is attached to a spring within the housing. The free end of the tape attaches to the window frame. Lift the window up and the spring expands; close it and the spring compresses.

To install a tape balance is not a simple matter. However, it can be done by someone without great experience.

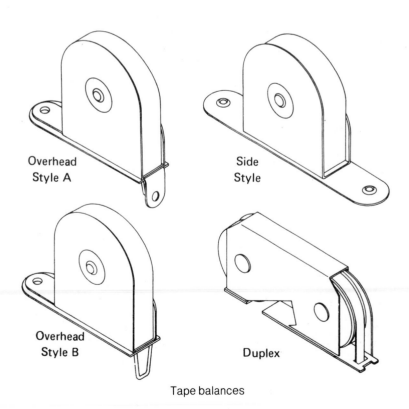

Overhead
Style A

Side
Style

Overhead
Style B

Duplex

Tape balances

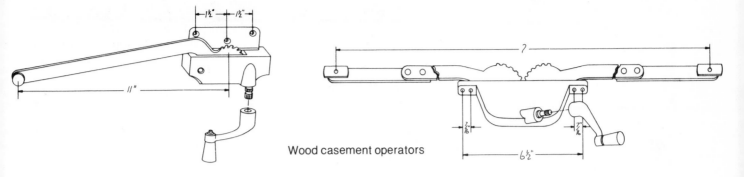

Wood casement operators

Replacement channel. Also consider replacement channels. A couple of companies make these. One is Quaker City Manufacturing Company.

The channels seem simple to install. The ropes or chains are cut, letting them drop into the sash well. This leaves a pulley on each side, which either must be pried out or banged in with a hammer. Any damage that is done to the frame doesn't matter; the channels cover the track up (Tip: You can provide a little more insulation by pouring chopped-up insulation into the wells.)

The stop molding is also removed and the window sash then lifted out. The two sashes are then set upright and the channels slipped over the edges and pushed back into the window frame. Channels are screwed to the frame, the stop molding reinstalled, and the window, after adjustments, is ready to work. Channels are spring loaded to press against the sides of the window sash, thus providing a tight seal while letting the sash ride freely and stop positively.

Quaker City makes these channels to cover 85 percent of standard 1⅜"-thick sash, whether operated by rope, chain, spring, or spiral-balanced sash. They will not fit sash that is 1⅜" thick or that weighs more than 25 pounds and is not full cut.

Another product by the same company is "take-out" windows. These require experience to install. The window must be modified a bit, and a spring-actuated channel must be installed that will regulate the way the window rides. The advantage is that the installed windows can be taken out easily for cleaning or painting.

If you'd rather just replace a damaged rope sash, it's advisable to use chain. This simply works better. However, as noted in the section on chain (pages 8–13), if your home is near a seashore or other area where moisture is abundant, then it's best to stick with rope. Moisture can rust and corrode sash chain, even bronze.

To install Quaker City channels, first remove the sash by taking out stop molding.

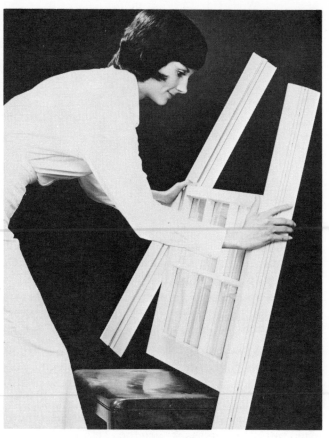

Place channels on the sash.

Replace the sash.

Replace the molding. It's not this easy, but these are the essential steps.

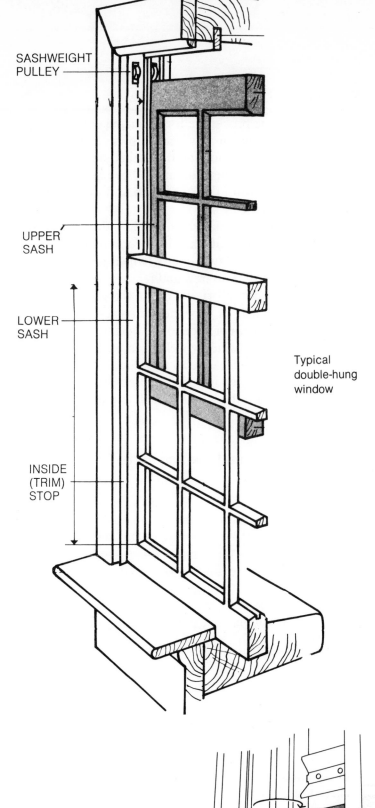

SASHWEIGHT
PULLEY

UPPER
SASH

LOWER
SASH

INSIDE
(TRIM)
STOP

Typical
double-hung
window

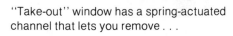

"Take-out" window has a spring-actuated
channel that lets you remove . . .

. . . the window by pressing to one side.

Windows

At any rate, the procedure for replacing chain or rope in the average double hung window is as follows:

1. Remove the stop molding (it's nailed on) with a chisel. Do this carefully because this molding will be replaced.

2. Tip out the bottom window sash and unhook the rope or chain attached to the top.

3. Let the chain or rope drop down into the window well.

4. Pull the window out, then look for a panel in the track. It is normally held on by two screws (which may be painted over so they're obscured). Unscrew and remove.

5. With panel cover off, take out the chain and rope and weight. Get new chain or rope the same size.

6. Attach new chain or rope to the weight.

7. Drop weight in window well, then pull chain or rope over pulley and attach the free end to the window.

8. Repeat the procedure described above (steps 1–7) on the other side, then slip the window back in place and reinstall the stop molding.

Jalousie Window and Awning Parts

Replacement parts are available for jalousie windows and awnings, but not normally in hardware stores. For jalousie parts, check the Yellow Pages for companies that make windows and sell to the retail trade. Do the same for awning parts—check stores that make these awnings. Fortunately, awning parts rarely require replacement. If you live in a rural area that has a large local hardware store, you may be able to get the parts. Otherwise, you can follow the procedure outlined earlier for window parts: Check out your local store, have the dealer show the part to a specialized jobber, or contact Blaine.

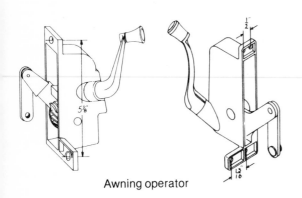

Awning operator

Wire

Wire comes in various gauges, with 10, 12, 14, 16, and 20 the most common gauges used around the home.

There are a couple of different kinds that are useful: single-strand drawn wire and twisted strand. Both types are galvanized for outdoor use. The first is a single piece of wire, while the latter contains three or four separate wire strands twisted together.

The twisted strand is probably most used. Typically, it's used as guy wire support and for dog runs. In the very light gauges—

18 and 20—it can be used for tying things, and hanging things such as Christmas wreaths or pictures. At these gauges it is very pliable, easy to bend, and easy to fasten. All you need to do is to drive a nail or screw into a material, then wrap the wire around it.

Another kind of wire is plastic coated. This is used for clothesline and is easy to keep clean by wiping it with a damp rag. It was mentioned in the section on rope and cord (pages 58–59).

Wire can be bought in coils or in packages, such as for hanging picture hooks.

SIZES OF WIRE

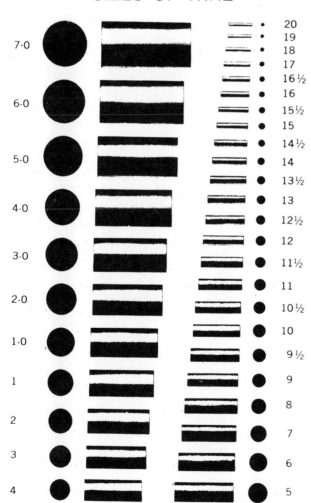

II

MINIATURE HARDWARE

Miniature Hardware

In recent years there has been a tremendous new interest in miniature hardware, perhaps more commonly known as dollhouse hardware (a name miniaturists abhor because it implies that grown-up people play with dolls). Indeed, marketing figures show that it is now the fifth most popular hobby in America.

When one speaks of miniatures, one means items that are on a scale of 1 inch to the foot; the item is one-twelfth the size of the actual item. While some companies sell miniature items bigger than this, it is generally regarded as incorrect. If you are going to collect, rules are required.

Today it is safe to say that the determined collector can get virtually anything that is actual size in miniature. Not too long ago, indeed, one company started selling miniature coffins. It is also possible to get all kinds of hardware and working electrical items, including house wiring. Perhaps the only area where the manufacturers have not duplicated life in miniature is in plumbing. One can buy fixtures—sink, tub, and toilet—but no one has yet come up with ones that actually work. Perhaps this is fortunate—just imagine changing a washer on a faucet one-twelfth the size of an actual washer!

There are two sources where one can get miniature hardware, from stores and from catalogues. Different kinds of stores are selling it. There are hobby shops, craft shops, and miniature shops that specialize in it, as well as toy stores and stores that specialize in something else—say, needlepoint.

Cir-Kit Concepts sells a clear plastic house. Note the flat bands of wire. Installed in a wooden dollhouse, these bands would be painted over. A transformer converts house voltage to the low voltage required.

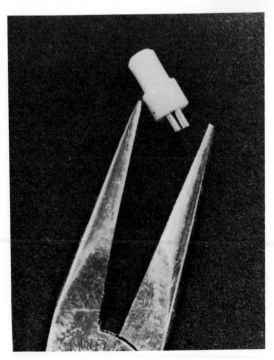

The relative size of miniatures can be seen here. The white object is a plug.

Nails used are perhaps the tiniest items of all.

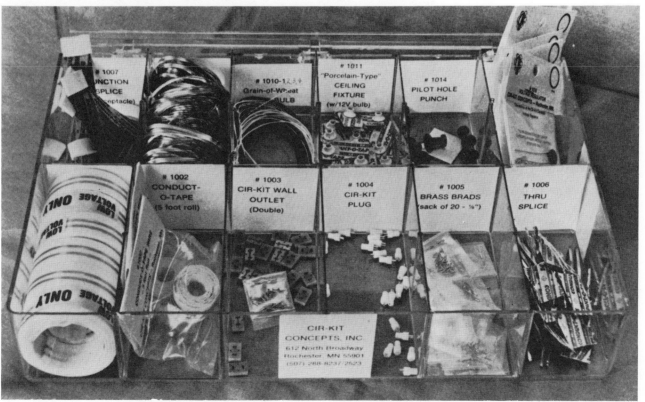

Other items sold

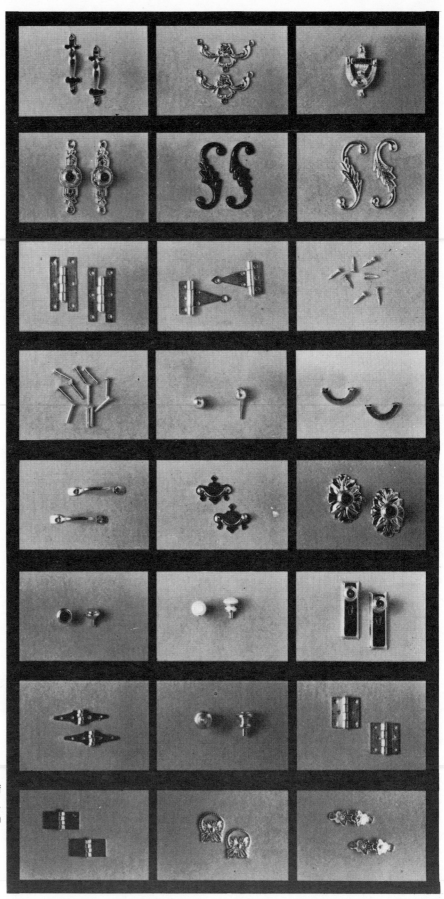

What is said to be the largest retailer of miniature hardware is Houseworks Ltd. The hardware items they sell are shown here.

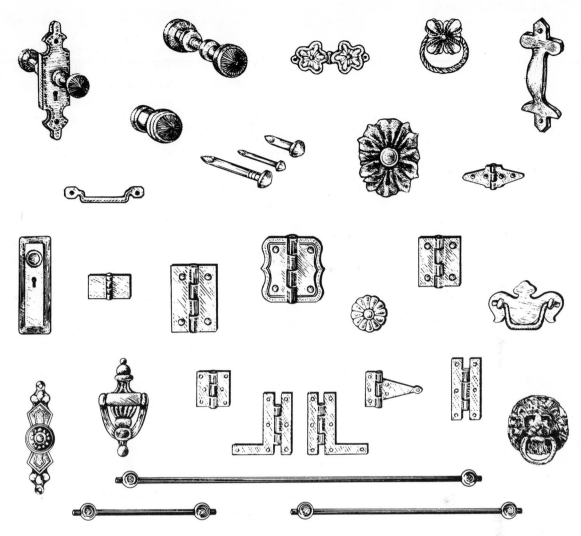

Another large manufacturer is Craft Creative Kits. Their hardware line is also shown here. Both Houseworks and Craft Creative Kits sell items that are on a scale of 1 inch to the foot.

There are also many different companies who sell it by mail. In general, the hardware from these stores—and we are sticking to hardware here—is either manufactured overseas in Germany or in Asia, chiefly Taiwan or custom made. The custom-made material is, of course, more expensive. But, as the saying goes, you get what you pay for.

BUYING TIPS

Before buying any hardware (or any miniature, for that matter), there are some important things to know. Miniature collecting is not cheap, and you can be bilked if you're not careful.

The catalogues themselves are overpriced in many instances; to be paying three or four dollars for what amounts to a fat brochure or some mimeographed sheets is not fair. On the other hand, the collector should probably make the investment, because the simple fact is that one can often get better prices from a catalogue than from a store. In one instance, for example, a dollhouse that was selling for $200 in a retail store—reduced from $300—was seen in a catalogue for $150.

I am speaking of *manufacturers'* catalogues. There are many retailers who will buy manufacturers' items, add their own markup, and put it in their own catalogue or stores. The author saw one case where manufacturers' prices were doubled and inflated ''handling'' charges were added.

Sometimes, too, the merchandise is inferior. There is no iron-clad way to avoid getting inferior merchandise. All I can recommend is that you carefully read the ads—or read between the lines—for signs of what is really being sold.

SOURCES

A book that should be a boon to miniature collectors was scheduled for publication as this was being written. Boynton and Associates is coming out with *The Miniatures Catalog,* which rounds up what is available nationwide in miniature buildings, building supplies and components, hardware, furniture, books and plans, decorating accessories, and tools. Names and addresses of manufacturers are listed, but Boynton wants to stress that they are selling a catalogue only—they're not a supplier of the items.

The Miniatures Catalog sells for $5.50 ($4.75 plus $.75 handling and postage). It is also available in miniatures outlets (check there first). The catalogue is 200 pages, 8½″ × 11½″, and includes a color section and many black-and-white illustrations of products. Boynton's address is Boynton and Associates, Clifton House, Clifton, Virginia 22024.

Following are the names of some manufacturers, prepared with the help of Boynton, either individuals or companies, who sell miniature hardware and electrical items by mail order. Some of the companies also sell their items in retail stores.

Miniature Hardware

Aaron Supply Company
435 Benefit Street
Pawtucket, Rhode Island 02861

Colonial Craftsmen Pewter Workshop
Division of Stieff Company
800 Wyman Park Drive
Baltimore, Maryland 21211

Craft, Incorporated
1930 County Street
South Attleboro, Maine 02703

The Village Smithy
RD #5. Hemlock Trail
Carmel, New York 10512

X-Acto
45–35 Van Dam Street
Long Island City, New York 11101

Evanscraft
306 Van Ness Avenue
Upland, California 91786

Illinois Hobbycraft, Inc.
Distributor Division
605 North Broadway
Aurora, Illinois 60606

Phillip J. Grande
513 East Orange Grove Avenue
Burbank, California 91501

Craft Creative Kits
Department 70
2200 Dean Street
Saint Charles, Illinois 60174

Clare Bell Brassworks
Nelsontool
P.O. Box 309
Southington, Connecticut 06489

Cir-Kit Concepts, Inc.
612 North Broadway
Rochester, Minnesota 55901

Two magazines that specialize in miniatures are

Nutshell News (four times a year)
P. O. Box 1144
La Jolla, California 92038
($5.50 per year)

The Miniature Collector (six times a year)
150 Fifth Avenue
New York, New York 10010
($9.97 per year)

III

ELECTRICAL
HARDWARE

How an Electrical System Works

A home's electrical system is like its plumbing system, but instead of water flowing through pipes, electricity flows through wires.

In order to flow, electricity requires a circuit: a closed loop that goes around and around. When this circuit is broken, the electricity stops flowing.

The circuit starts at the power company, where electricity is generated by the action of huge magnets. From there it flows through high-tension wires to a service line that leads into the home; this line is called the service entrance cable. The line goes through the electric meter, which records its use; electricity continues to flow to the fuse box or circuit breaker panel. From there it flows through house circuit wires to receptacles where the power is tapped off for use by electrical devices.

Let's follow the path of one circuit. From the circuit breaker or fuse box the electricity flows through a black wire (usually called the hot leg), through the device—say, the filament of a light bulb—and then back along the neutral or white wire to the circuit breaker or fuse box and then to the power station. All this happens instantaneously.

In practice, most people will only be concerned with the house circuit: the flow of electricity from the breaker or fuse box.

Power coming through the circuit may be 120 volts or 240 volts. One black wire or hot leg carries 120; if there is another hot wire, and there almost always is, it will be colored red and will also carry 120 volts, for a total of 240. The wire that carries 120 volts is connected to lamps and similar devices, whereas high voltage—240—is required by major appliances.

FLUORESCENT FIXTURE
100 Watts

ELECTRIC BLANKET
135-200 Watts

CEILING LIGHT
100 Watts

VACUUM CLEANER
400 Watts

GENERAL PURPOSE CIRCUITS-115v
#14 Wire, 15 amps or
#12 Wire, 20 amps

Typical circuit in the home. Devices use watts of power.

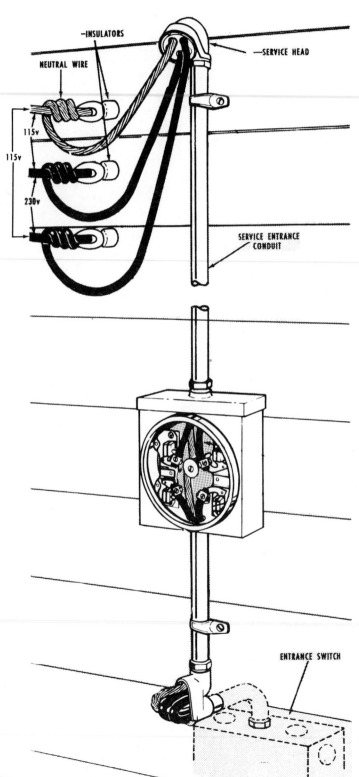

—INSULATORS

NEUTRAL WIRE

—SERVICE HEAD

115v

115v

230v

SERVICE ENTRANCE CONDUIT

ENTRANCE SWITCH

Power comes into your house from lines tapped off power company lines. The illustration shows components used in some installations. In this installation there would be two hot wires, each carrying 110 (also called 115) volts.

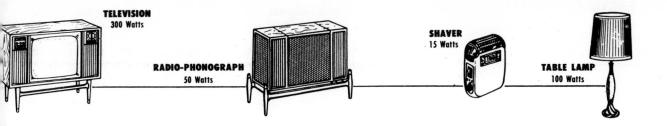

TELEVISION
300 Watts

RADIO-PHONOGRAPH
50 Watts

SHAVER
15 Watts

TABLE LAMP
100 Watts

Grounding

For safety, all electrical systems must be grounded—that is, connected to the earth.

To understand grounding, you can forget the normal electrical circuit. The ground is simply a separate metallic path for the electricity to the earth in case the device you are using, such as a toaster or appliance, develops an electrical leak. If a leak occurred and there was no grounding system, electricity would electrify the appliance. You would touch it and get a shock.

Fortunately, though, metal is a much better conductor, or carrier, of electricity than a human body. So if a metallic path is open to it, the electricity will take it. If it isn't, it won't.

Electrical systems are grounded in a variety of ways. There may be a separate wire—copper—connected to the receptacle or switch that runs to and is attached to a grounding bar in the fuse, or circuit breaker panel, box. A copper wire or rod leads, in turn, to another metal object—usually the water meter—which is in contact with the ground, or it may be a metal rod buried in the earth.

In other cases the path to the earth is along the outside of the metal cable—BX cable is one such. If a leak develops in the device, the errant electricity would flow from it through the receptacle, which would in turn be connected to the BX cable. Normally, then, errant electricity would go back to the fuse box or circuit breaker panel which is connected to the earth. It should be emphasized that the same electrical device can be grounded in various ways; all of them are fine. As long as there is that metallic path, one method is as good as another.

Terms

A number of terms are used throughout the electrical products section.

Volt. This is the unit used to measure the pressure at which electricity flows through wires. In normal house wiring, as mentioned, it would be 117–120 volts, commonly referred to as 110; or 240, commonly referred to as 220 v. The lower figures are used because in practice voltage can vary, but normally the lower amounts come into the house.

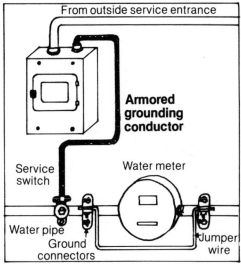

One way of grounding electricity. Errant electricty would travel to the ground through water pipes.

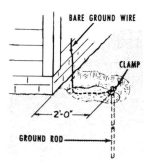

Another way of grounding electricity. Here electricity would go through the rod into the ground.

Ampere. Also called amps, or amperage, this describes the rate at which electrical current flows through a circuit. A normal circuit for lights is 15 amps; larger appliances use 20 to 50 amps, and one entire circuit may be needed for just one appliance.

Watt. This is the unit that shows electrical power drain, in terms of both voltage and amperage. In so many words, it describes the amount of electricity one uses. To determine how much electricity is used, you multiply the number of volts a device uses times its amperage. For example, a toaster might be rated at 6 amps, and if the voltage is 110 (as it is in some systems), it would use 660 watts (6 amps times 110 volts). To calculate your electrical bill, the utility company charges so much per watt per hour—1,000 watts for one hour equals 1,000 watt-hours, which equals 1 kilowatt-hour.

Circuit breaker. This is a safety device that shuts off the flow of electrical current if the wires are carrying too much current. It becomes overloaded when the electricity being used by the total number of devices in operation exceeds the amperage capacity of the circuit. A fuse serves the same purpose. If the current flow were not shut off, the excess current could burn up the wires and start a fire.

Electric service panel. This is the common name for the fuse box and circuit breaker panel. It is normally located in the basement of your home.

Short circuit. This is caused when, for some reason, the circuit the electricity takes is shorter than it should be, that is, it doesn't travel all the way through the hot wire, into the device, and back to the panel.

Alternating current. This is the type of power used in all farm and home wiring systems. It is commonly called AC.

Calculating Your Circuit Capacity

It's a time-consuming process, but it's an excellent idea to know the capacity of the various circuits in your home. Knowing the total capacity of each will enable you to use electrical devices and yet not overload the circuit.

To do this, first turn on all the lights in your house and plug lamps into receptacles normally used by small appliances such as toasters. Down at the fuse or breaker box turn off one breaker or unscrew one fuse. Check to see which lights go off. Mark them down (a floor plan of your house showing receptacles helps), showing the wattage of each device used on that circuit; remember to mark down the wattage of appliances that have been replaced by lights. The wattage is usually on the appliance housing.

When you've added up all the wattages, call this circuit number 1 and mark the total wattage after it. If the circuit is 15 amperes and totals more than 1,650 watts, that circuit is just about overloaded, because 15 amps times 110 volts has 1,650 watts capacity. A 20-amp circuit should not handle more than 2,200 watts, assuming that everything is turned on all at once.

Repeat the procedure for the other circuits (the average house usually has nine or ten). Once you know the answers, you'll know exactly what you can or cannot add, as long as you know the wattage of each device to be used.

In some cases, the wattage of a device will not be marked on it. Rather, you will get the amperage. To convert it to wattage, just multiply by 110 volts. A 7-amp device, for example, would draw 770 watts.

It should be remembered that what you are calculating is the *total* capacity of particular circuits. It may well be that not every receptacle or light switch will be on at one time. So, for example, if you know that your number 1 circuit only normally has two lights used on it, then you could likely use a small-wattage appliance without overloading it.

Keep the capacities of the circuits handy. The best place is down by the fuse box or circuit breaker panel. You'll know instantly what the capacity of a circuit is when you want to add a device.

SAFETY TIPS

Electricity, of course, can be dangerous, and there are a number of things you should observe when dealing with it.

First, no matter what you are working on (except a portable device that you unplug), turn off the current at the fuse box or circuit breaker panel. Before doing this, plug a light into the receptacle. When you turn off the circuit, the light should go out.

As a double check when working on electrical devices a circuit tester can give you an added measure of security. It comes with instructions for use.

Don't buy any electrical product unless you see the UL label on it. Otherwise, you can't be sure it's safe.

If you are working on a ceiling fixture, the same thing can be done. Turn the switch on and watch to see if the light comes on. If the fixture is not operative, you can buy a simple testing device called a circuit tester to ensure that it's dead, assuming you don't know which circuit fuse or breaker controls it. The circuit tester can also be used to double check a receptacle even when you can identify the fuse or breaker that controls it.

To ensure electrical safety, the National Electrical Code was established by fire insurance companies that details safe procedures and devices to use when doing any electrical work. Many local communities have adopted this code as their own. However, before doing any work, check with the local authorities to make sure that what you're doing is legal; there may be variations in the code. And after it is completed, have the job inspected by the local authorities for safety. If you do not, and a fire results, and the insurance company can prove that your work was responsible for the fire, your homeowner's insurance can be voided.

Finally, before you buy *any* device or wire, make sure that it has the Underwriters' Laboratories' seal on it. The seal does not mean that UL approves the device per se, just that it is "listed," meaning that UL has tested the device and has found that it has passed acceptable safety standards. Buying a device that does not have the UL label on it is asking for trouble.

Fuses

Fuses work on a simple principle. Each is designed to handle a specified amount of current. When the current exceeds the amount that the fuse is designed for, a metal linkage in the fuse melts: The current stops flowing before the overloaded wires can heat up. A fuse, then, is a safety device, and the do-it-yourselfer should never try to circumnavigate it.

Two different kinds of fuses are commonly used around the home: plug-in and cartridge. By far the most common is the plug-in type (which, in a way, is a misnomer, since it screws in place). In essence, it consists of a housing with a threaded end, the linkage inside, and a tiny glass window through which one can check to see if the fuse has "blown"; that is, the linkage has broken either because of an overload or because of a short circuit. Technically, plug fuses are referred to as Edison-base types, the name being taken from the Edison panel or load center they screw into.

Plug-In Fuses

Standard plug-in fuses are usually available in small packages, but dealers will commonly break open the package to sell you one or two. Fuses are available at hardware stores and, of course, at electrical supply stores. If you are ever caught with a blown fuse at a time when the usual stores are not open, try a supermarket or large drugstore. Many times these carry fuses for just such emergencies.

Standard plug-in fuse

Perhaps of all the fuses available the standard plug-in fuse is the safest to use. Electricians will tell you that they never fail (unlike circuit breakers, whose internal mechanism can malfunction).

Plug-in fuses range in size from 5 to 30 amps: 5, 15, 20, 25, and 30. Smaller sizes than 5 amp can also be gotten. Fifteen amps is what is normally used for the lighting circuits in the house. Large appliances such as air-conditioners and other heavy-amperage-drawing devices use 20-amp, 25-amp, or 30-amp fuses.

Time-Delay Fuses

Time-delay fuses (Fusetron is one brand name) won't open when hit by a surge of current. This is a good fuse to use where a motor is used. The starting current won't affect it.

Time-delay fuse

Renewable Fuses

Renewable fuses look like the standard fuses, but they differ in that they can be reset after they blow. They have a heating element, which separates when the circuit is carrying too much current. To reset the fuse, however, you just push in a little cylinder projecting from the top of the fuse; you needn't take the fuse out to do this.

Circuit saver from Sears can be reset by hitting the button.

While this reset feature is convenient, some electricians note that the fuse is subject to malfunction: The interior mechanism can short itself and the fuse won't blow when it should.

Renewable fuses are available at hardware stores and electrical supply houses. They are available in the same sizes as the standard plug-in fuse and will cost around 50 percent more.

Type-S fuse (Fustat)

Type-S Plug-in Fuses

These fuses, commonly called Fustats (a brand name), differ markedly from the three just discussed. They consist of two parts: a threaded adapter, which screws into the electrical panel, and the fuse proper, which screws into the adapter.

The big advantage of this fuse is that it is tamper-proof. Other plug-in fuses are interchangeable in size; ones of different amperage will screw into the same fuse holder. Fustats are sized so that a specific size fuse—say 15 amps—may only be used with its particular adapter. That is, if the adapter for a 15-amp fuse is screwed in place, it will only accept its corresponding 15-amp fuse part. This, of course, makes it impossible to use a larger fuse where a smaller fuse is called for, which unfortunately is an expediency some electricians will take, thereby rendering unsafe the circuit supposedly protected by that fuse. Such a feature makes the type-S fuse particularly sensible for someone who rents out his property to tenants.

All plug-in fuses have their specific amperage-carrying capacity marked on the top. However, type-S fuses are also color coded: The adapter and fuse proper are the same color so that components of different fuses can't get confused.

Type-S fuses are available in the same sizes and stores as mentioned for other fuses.

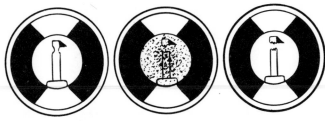

Fuses tell a story when they blow: *left,* good fuse, *Center,* Short-circuit— blackened window, *right,* overloaded fuse, clear but linkage melted.

Fuse puller. This should be used with cartridge fuses.

Cartridge Fuses

These fuses are less used in the home, but they are used. They are designed for handling large power demands—above 30 amps and 220 volts for such things as appliances and air-conditioning equipment, where a separate fuse is required to control a particular appliance circuit.

In appearance, the standard cartridge fuse looks something like a shotgun shell casing. It is installed between clips in the switch on the appliance. Inside, the fuse functions essentially like any other fuse: Current runs through a metal linkage; when the current exceeds the capacity of the linkage, it breaks.

One type available is the "one-time" type. There is a linkage inside that melts, breaking the circuit, in case of overload or short circuit. Then the fuse is replaced.

Another type of cartridge fuse has a replaceable linkage. When the linkage burns out, you unscrew the ends of the cartridge, remove the old linkage, and replace it with a new one. Also available are cartridge fuses with "knife blades"—projecting metal ends. These are used for amperages above 65, such as main fuses.

Cartridge fuses are available at hardware stores and, of course, at electrical supply houses.

Circuit Breakers

Circuit breakers can be used in place of fuses. Indeed, they are more popular. The reason is convenience: A flip of a switch can get a circuit operative again, rather than physically unscrewing a fuse and screwing a new one back in place.

At the heart of the construction of the typical circuit breaker is a bimetallic strip with a couple of springs and contact points. When a circuit becomes overloaded or another electrical malfunction takes place, this bimetallic strip bends and pulls away from contact points, breaking the circuit. The electrical flow shuts down.

The exterior of a circuit breaker typically consists of a series of toggle switches. When the circuit is shut down, the switch that controls the circuit indicates this by moving partly away from the *On* position and toward *Off*, words which are imprinted on the breaker. After correcting the reason for the malfunction (the same thing you should do with a fuse), you simply flip the switch all the way to the *Off* position, then to *On*. Inside the device the bimetallic strip reconnects the circuit, and electricity flows.

Top, renewable fuse; *bottom,* standard cartridge fuse

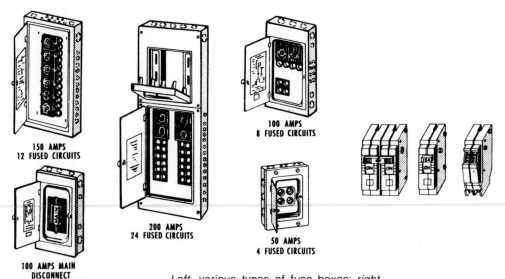

150 AMPS
12 FUSED CIRCUITS

100 AMPS MAIN
DISCONNECT

200 AMPS
24 FUSED CIRCUITS

100 AMPS
8 FUSED CIRCUITS

50 AMPS
4 FUSED CIRCUITS

Left, various types of fuse boxes; *right,* individual circuit breakers

Circuit breakers are rated according to the amperage they can handle and are available from 5 amps to hundreds of amps. In the typical house a 100-amp service is considered the minimum.

Two types of breakers are common: those that are snapped or pushed into slots for installation and those that are screwed into place. Most come with toggle-type switches; others have buttons that are pushed in order to reset them.

If you want to replace a circuit breaker, you must sometimes get a direct-replacement unit from the same manufacturer. To find out the name, check on the door or panel housing itself. In many cases, however, circuit breakers are interchangeable. GE, for example, can be substituted for ITE. To be sure that you get the right size, the best bet is to bring the old breaker to the supply house.

INSTALLATION TIPS

If you want to replace a circuit breaker that's bad (you can tell this simply because a circuit will go dead and the handle on the breaker won't trip), it is not a difficult job. Basically, as mentioned, it will either be snapped or screwed into place. However, the electric service panel cover must be removed to install the unit, and this exposes a lot of live wires. Make sure that you pull the main fuse, or trip the main breaker, as the case may be, before getting involved in the operation.

Circuit breakers are generally available at better stocked hardware stores and electrical supply houses.

Electrical Boxes

Wherever wires are stripped of insulation and hooked onto terminal screws, such as on a receptacle or switch or joined to a fixture, or where they are joined for the purpose of changing the direction of the wire, they must be housed in a metal or plastic box for safety. No raw wire should be left exposed.

Boxes are available in various shapes and sizes. The National Electric Code puts restrictions on how many wires may be in a particular size box because crowding of wires can be a safety hazard.

Boxes have either of two arrangements for accepting wires. The box may have a number of knockouts—holes with removable metal discs—or the holes may be open. Inside the box there may not be clamps for holding the cable that is passed through these holes.

For house wiring, holes and knockouts are normally ½" in diameter. Removing a knockout is simple. You can hold a screwdriver against the disc and rap the screwdriver with a hammer, then pull it out with pliers. Better boxes come with discs that can be pried out with a screwdriver. If you accidentally remove the wrong knockout, there are plugs of various kinds that can be used to close the hole. The idea, again, is to have solid metal or plastic all around the wires.

To attach conduit (metal pipe through which wires are pushed) to boxes, connectors are used; in some cases cable is also hooked on with connectors. These fasten to the cable and the box and will be covered in more detail in the sections on working with wire.

Four-inch octagon box without cable clamps. This would be used with conduit. The knockouts would be removed, connectors attached in the holes, then the conduit passed through and secured by the connectors.

Boxes with Clamps

On boxes with clamps, you insert the cable in the hole in the box, through the clamps, and turn down screws to fasten it in place.

Covers for boxes are bought separately to fit particular boxes. There are a variety of these. Some of them are basically rims of metal with an opening in the middle through which the switch or outlet is accessible. Other types are designed for boxes that are mounted on the wall surface, such as on a basement wall. Here the covers are solid pieces of metal with turned-over edges to fit over the box, with cutouts in the cover through which the outlet slots are accessible. These kinds may be either square or round. Finally, some covers are solid metal. These

Same type of box with clamps. Here set-screws on the clamps are tightened on the cable.

Covers for various style boxes

Box for new work. Bracket would be nailed to stud.

would be used on junction boxes to cover up spliced wires; a fixture with a metal base that covers an open box may also be considered a cover. Boxes also come with or without plaster ears. These are brackets on the top and bottom of the box that may be adjusted forward or backward. The ears grip the surface of the wall material when the box is installed so it can't fall into the wall.

Box, cover, and receptacle or switch go together simply by screwing the parts together through standardized threaded holes that match. The adjustable ears let you bring the box flush with the wall so that the switch or receptacle face can be flush too.

INSTALLATION TIPS

Boxes may be mounted in a variety of ways, but they can be basically broken down into two types: Those designed to be mounted where framing members are exposed—new work—and those that can be mounted where the walls enclose the framing—old work.

For new work there are boxes that come with brackets, which are nailed directly to studs. The box may be mounted either to the side or in front of the framing member, wherever you want the electrical device located.

Other boxes come with adjustable brackets. The brackets are attached to the sides of the box, then telescoped out, and their ends nailed to studs or joists. Raco Company also makes boxes with the brackets already attached. This can speed up the fastening of the box between the framing members.

While metal studs are mainly used in commercial buildings, some contractors use them for home building, and they are available to do-it-yourselfers. One manufacturer is Gould Inc., Electrical Components Division. Here a slotted bracket is simply screwed to the stud and the box slid along the bracket until it is in the desired position; it is then locked into place.

You have a choice of ways for mounting boxes to old work. Which one you use depends to a large degree on whether the wall is plaster-and-lath (wetwall) construction or drywall (Sheetrock) construction.

Some boxes, for example may be mounted by cutting a hole in the wall the size of the box, then cutting out portions of the lath, laying the box in place, and screwing it on the lath by the ears. Unless you are careful, you can cut the opening oversize. One way to solve this problem is with an oversize wall plate, as noted in the section on wall plates (page 145).

For drywall, other means of mounting are necessary because there is no lath, and Sheetrock is not solid enough to support screws or nails nor is it practical to use other fasteners. One way is with a box with clamps on the side. The box is inserted into the wall, then the screws on the side of it tightened and the clamps expand to grip the wall from the backside while the plaster ears grip the front.

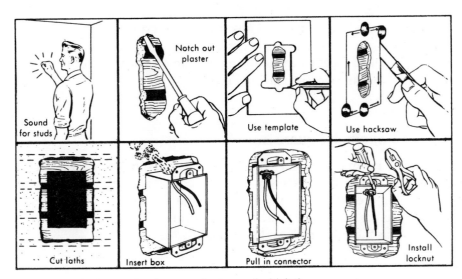

Sound for studs · Notch out plaster · Use template · Use hacksaw · Cut laths · Insert box · Pull in connector · Install locknut

One method of mounting box to plaster wall with lath

Another way is with Madison clips. These are two pieces of sheet metal with tabs (in outline they each look like battleships and have been nicknamed that by electricians). After the box is installed so that its ears overlap the front of the wall, a clip is worked in on each side of the box (short side down) so that it grips the wall from behind at the top and bottom. The tabs on it are then bent around the front edges of the box to hold it securely in position. Another clip is installed the same way on the other side. If using these, take care to make sure that the tabs lie flat inside the box. If they touch parts of the device, short circuits can result.

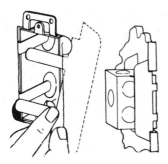

Madison clips. Plaster ears on box grip the outside of the wall so box can't fall in; Madison clips are slipped in on sides of box, then bent over so that the box can't fall out (*right*, view is from inside the wall).

Gem Boxes

While there are many different boxes available, and they are perhaps interesting to read about, in practice only a few specific kinds will be required by most do-it-yourselfers. At the head of the parade is the Gem box.

No one seems to know where the term *Gem box* came from. It is not a brand name but rather a generic term for a commonly used box produced by a number of different manufacturers. At

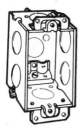

Gem box. It is available to accept one, two, or more receptacles and switches.

any rate, it is a metal box that is 2″ wide, 3″ high, and 2½″ deep. It comes with or without plaster ears. Like other boxes, gem boxes with ears are to keep the box level with the surface of plaster, plasterboard, or other wall material. If the box has no ears, it is used on new work and will have holes in it for nailing to studs. It is also available with clamps on the side to secure the box to the wall, but the most popular device for doing this —and the easiest—is Madison clips, described earlier.

Gem boxes can be "ganged"—sides removed and the boxes hooked together to handle more than one switch or outlet. They also come larger than 2½″ deep.

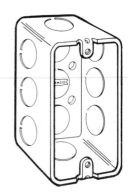

Handy box. This is useful when you have limited space; it also has rounded corners so that it can't snag anyone.

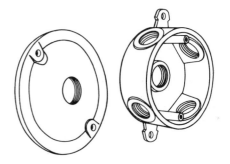

This is a fixture box with aluminum weatherproof cover. It is threaded to accept a fixture.

Four-Inch Square Box

In some situations there won't be enough depth in the wall to mount a Gem box. In this case consider using the four-inch-square box. This is 4″ square, but is only 1½″ deep (it also comes 2⅛″). The switch or outlet can be mounted, and the box has the cubic-inch capacity to house the wires.

Handy Box

This box is indeed handy. It is for surface mounting of switches and receptacles. The big advantage is that the corners are rounded. Someone can bump into it and not get scratched, as might happen with regular boxes.

Weatherproof Boxes

For exterior use there are waterproof boxes that come in either single or duplex form. These may be cast aluminum or malleable iron. The aluminum types are recommended anywhere that abuse is not expected, such as in a garden area; they are also cheaper than the iron types. If you are installing a switch or receptacle in an area where damage may be incurred—say, a driveway—the iron type is better because it can take a hard blow.

Covers may be of the screw or snap type. The screw type is relatively permanent. To use the receptacle, the screw must be removed in order to take off the cover. This type, obviously, should be used only where you would expect only occasional use of the receptacle or switch.

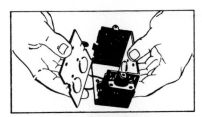

Snap-type cover. Just flip the lids, and the receptacles are accessible for plugging in devices.

Some boxes have removable sides enabling them to be linked together to form one large box.

On the snap-type cover you flip up a small cover, or covers, which exposes the switch or receptacle. This is for use in areas where the switch or receptacle will be used frequently.

Most outdoor light fixtures come with ½″ pipe threads (male) that attach to the box by screwing into a threaded portion (female) in the box.

Wire

Wires for electrical purposes are called conductors, simply because they conduct electricity. Actually, wire is a misnomer, because you don't buy bare metal. Rather, the wire—the metal—comes covered with insulation, usually plastic. The conductor may be either solid metal or twisted strands; solid conductors are used in standard house wiring, while the stranded conductors are used in appliances and large-capacity wires.

The conductors may be copper or aluminum. Here we will discuss copper. At this writing there is a controversy over whether aluminum wire is safe. At any rate, wire with copper conductors is available in all the forms needed for various uses around the home.

Wire is commonly spoken of in terms of number, which refers to the diameter of the wire. The *larger* the number, the

ACTUAL WIRE SIZE OF COPPER CONDUCTORS

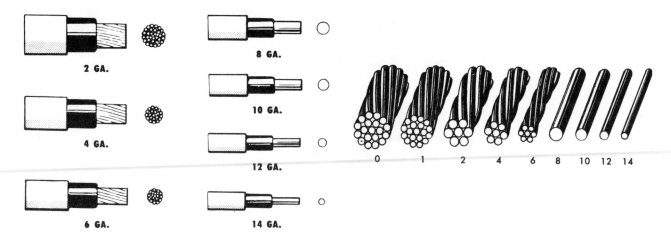

smaller the wire. Number 38 wire is a little thicker than a human hair. As the numbers increase, the wire gets thinner: For example, no. 18 wire is about the diameter of a pencil lead; no. 14 is about the size of the head of a pin. Going down the scale further, no. 2 wire has the diameter of a pencil. And it keeps getting bigger, with the numbered designations changing after no. 00 to1/0, 2/0, 3/0, 4/0, and so forth, as the wire continues to get bigger.

The bigger the wire, the more current it can carry. The do-it-yourselfer will only be concerned with relatively few wires. The most commonly used in house wiring are nos. 14 and 12 wire whereas nos. 18, 16, and 15 are common for appliance cords. If you are very handy, you will also be involved with nos. 3 and 1 wire, for service entrance hookups, say, which require beefy wires.

Insulated wire is also classified by letter according to the type of covering or insulation used (you would need to vary this according to whether you are using wire in a wet, dry, or damp location, as these terms are defined by the National Electrical Code). Type SPT is used for lamps, radios, and the like. Types SV and SVT are used on vacuum cleaners. Type SJ is used on appliance cords. These are wires for dry locations.

Wires are also colored, and each color designates the purpose of the wire. Black wire is used for the hot leg—it carries the current to the electrical device. White wire is neutral. Ground wire is bare.

There are two popular types of wire for house circuits. Each comes in cable form, which means that wires are grouped together.

Romex Cable

One popular type is called nometallic sheathed, or NM, cable. It consists of a flattish thermoplastic jacket with two or three insulated wires, each covered with insulation and wrapped with spiral paper tape and a paper-covered copper ground wire. The most popular trade name is Romex.

The National Electrical Code restricts the use of it to places that are always dry and that won't be subject to salt, oxidation, or other attacks from corrosion. This means, in so many words, enclosed by house walls.

Romex cable is lightweight and easy to use and cut. Although it is flexible it is also stiff enough to make it easy to snake through walls. It comes in 250′ rolls, but you can get it cut to any length you wish.

Armored Cable

Armored cable, commonly known by the name BX, is another popular flexible cable. This consists of two or three insulated wires, or conductors, each of which is wrapped in spiral layers of tough paper and all of them running inside a galvanized steel casing. Two-wire BX will have one black and one white wire but no ground wire. However, all BX has is a bonding wire, which runs along its length. The casing of the cable becomes the ground wire, but the bond wire serves as a backup in case the armor breaks.

BX cable is for use in the interior of the house, usually where you know it will be exposed to some physical abuse, such as on basement walls. It is not as flexible as Romex and is consequently more difficult to use.

THHN Wire

Another commonly used wire is type THHN, no. 14, wire (it handles 15 amps). This is covered with nylon. Lengths of it are used when wiring fluorescent fixtures. A length of it is run from the junction box to the fluorescent fixture, where it is joined to the black and white leads of the wire with wire nuts (for futher details, see page 128).

AF Wire

Type AF wire is used for wiring recessed ceiling fixtures. It is an asbestos-covered wire that can withstand high heat.

Recessed lighting fixtures may use 150-watt bulbs, and the rising heat would adversely affect other types of wire.

If you need to bury wires in the ground, you can use direct burial cable. There may be one, two, or more wires encased in a vinyl jacket; usually there is no ground line. It is called UF cable. This cable comes in various sizes, normally to carry 10 to 60 amps.

Service entrance cable is, just as its name implies, specifically made for use in service entrances: It is used to connect the electric meter to the house panel and the meter to the Edison Weather Head, the device into which the feed lines come from the power company lines. This material, also plastic, will handle from 45 to 200 amps.

BUYING TIPS

Wire is available in hardware stores and electrical supply stores and is commonly available. If you are only going to be needing a small amount of wire, you can pick it up at your hardware store. However, you are likely to get a better buy on longer pieces at an electrical supply outlet. There, also, the counterman is more likely to be able to provide you with wiring tips for your specific installation.

Conduit

There are some jobs where you may want to use conduit, which is the name for pipe through which the individual insulated wires are pulled. There are two major types: thin-wall and heavy-wall.

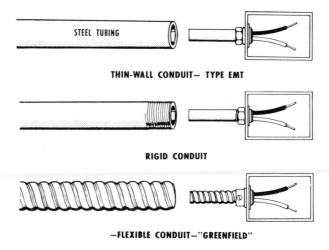

STEEL TUBING

THIN-WALL CONDUIT— TYPE EMT

RIGID CONDUIT

—FLEXIBLE CONDUIT—"GREENFIELD"

Thin-wall conduit. Thin-wall conduit, also called EMT (for electric metallic tubing), is thin-walled pipe that comes in inside diameters of from ½″ to 4″ and even larger, and in 10′ lengths; the ½″ size is most common. It commonly comes in light steel form.

EMT is normally used in areas where it must be exposed, such as along a garage wall for workshop wiring or for outdoor lighting runs. It should not be buried in the ground or exposed to abuse. Thin-wall may be bent with a special bender.

Heavy-wall conduit. Heavy-wall, or rigid, conduit, commonly comes galvanized, in the same diameters as thin-wall. It may be installed where it is exposed to the elements, in danger of physical abuse, and underground. For example, it could be buried under a lawn where it may be run over by a lawnmower. One use might be to run it from the home to a separate room addition.

Another type of conduit is the flexible type. It is generally called Greenfield, and looks like BX (armored cable), having a hollow, spiral-style metal jacket, but its diameter is larger, to allow wires to be pulled through. Thin-wall and rigid are not, as mentioned, normally used inside the home; Greenfield can be. It can be inserted in small holes in the wall; normally the only holes required will be those used later for outlet boxes. Greenfield is installed just like BX.

Plastic conduit. Finally, there is rigid plastic conduit—PVC (polyvinyl chloride). This is easier to use than its rigid metal counterpart (it's easily cut with a hacksaw) and is cheaper. It may be buried underground but, of course, will not take a damaging blow the way metal will.

There are limits to how many wires may be pulled through a conduit. It depends on the diameter of the pipe, of course, and the size of the wires. You should check with the local electrical inspector to find out exactly how many may be used. In general, ½″ conduit allows 7 conductors, while ¾″ allows 12.

While installing thin-wall and rigid conduit in existing installations would require opening up walls and ceilings, it might be considered for new installations. (Fittings are available to let you turn the conduit in any direction.) Later, if you want to add more wire, it can be a simple matter to pull it through the already installed conduit. Realize, though, that installing it in any structure is going to involve much drilling and sawing through framing members.

Staple

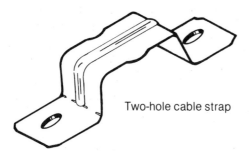

Two-hole cable strap

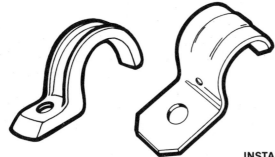

One-hole straps for conduit and cable

Fasteners for Cable and Conduit

Cable usually runs inside house walls and ceilings, but wherever it emerges into the open (such as on an open basement ceiling), it must be fastened in place; conduit must also be fastened. The most popular fastener for cable and flexible conduit is the staple, which is available in various sizes. You can use the same size staple for working with cable up to no. 10 (30-amp capacity), which will cover most situations.

Staples are driven into place with a hammer, but some people find this awkward to work with. A popular alternative—and definitely for use with rigid conduit—is the one-hole or two-hole metal cable strap, which is placed around the cable or rigid conduit and nails driven into the hole (or holes) of the strap. The two-hole strap makes for a more secure job, but both make for a neater job than staples, and you are able to shape the cables better with a strap than with a staple. One-hole types cost less than the two-hole type.

Straps are available in a variety of sizes. You select the same size as the conduit. If you are using ½″ conduit, get a ½″ strap, and so on.

INSTALLATION TIPS FOR STAPLES AND STRAPS

Staples should be installed over cable every 4′; one should also be used within 1′ of a junction box to guard against the conduit pulling free.

For fastening thin-wall, heavy-wall, or plastic conduit, straps work best. These should be used every 5′; and there should be one within 1′ of a junction box.

As to whether to use staples or straps, some electricians follow this rule: Staples are used inside the house, straps outside.

To make fastening conduit easier and more secure on various kinds of siding, follow these tips:

Brick and other masonry. A plastic or fiber plug with a no. 10 sheet metal screw works well. My preference is plastic: It's cheaper than fiber and grips the screw better. To use a fiber or lead plug, use a ³⁄₁₆″ carbide bit to drill a 1¼″ hole. Insert the plug, lay the conduit in place, then the strap, and turn the screw through the strap hole (or holes if you use the two-hole type) into the plug.

Cedar or asbestos. Here use no. 10 sheet metal screws; they grip much better than regular wood screws because their threads go all the way up to the head.

Aluminum siding and metal siding. Here punch a hole with an awl, then use a sheet metal screw. This method works on up to ³⁄₁₆″ gauge siding.

Wood. Use the sheet metal screw. Here, too, this type will hold better than the regular wood screw.

INSTALLATION TIPS FOR BX CABLE

BX cable can be cut as needed with a fine-toothed hacksaw. The cable should be held firmly and the saw held at a right angle to the armored spirals. Cut through one spiral, taking care not to damage the wires. When finished, grasp the cable on both sides of the cut and twist to separate the pieces. Expose about 8″ of wire for making a connection.

For safety, a fiber bushing must be pushed into the cut end of the cable. Otherwise, the raw metal edge could cut the wire insulation, resulting in a short circuit. To insert the bushing, unwrap the paper a few turns from under the armor, then jerk it to tear it off. Stick the bushing firmly in place, first bending the bonding wire back and tightly around the armor.

At some point BX cable will find its way to an electrical device—receptacle, outlet, fixture—in a box. There are various fittings available which will vary depending on the needs of the job.

Most Gem boxes, as mentioned in the section on electrical boxes (page 119), have a built-in clamp to accept the BX. Simply stick the cable through the knockout hole in the side of the box, set the BX in the clamp, and tighten the set screw to secure it. If you are connecting BX to an electric service panel, you'd use a separate connector of the proper size. Tightness is of utmost importance. Loose connections are probably the greatest cause of electrical malfunctions.

Working with BX: First, cut the cable on an angle. Twist the armor off. Insert fiber bushing, bending bond wire (not shown) around armor. Slip on connector. Slip connector into box and tighten locknut. When you use boxes with cable clamps, you don't need connectors. (Clamp has indentation to grip BX armor).

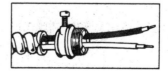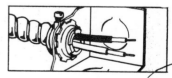

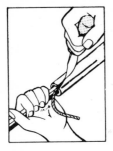

Working with Romex: Strip insulation carefully. Insert like BX into box and tighten. Romex can also, it should be remembered, be anchored to clamp-type boxes.

Connectors for cable and conduit: *Top,* box connector for thin-wall conduit; *center,* coupling for EMT; *bottom,* Romex and BX box connectors.

INSTALLATION TIPS FOR ROMEX CABLE

Fastening Romex to a box is essentially the same as for BX. First, use a sharp knife or cable ripper to cut back the insulation about 8", making your cut parallel to the wires. Take care not to damage the wires.

Slip the wires through the knockout and secure the cable by running down the setscrews on the built-in clamp. All boxes with clamps have a $^{19}\!/_{32}$" tapped grounding hole; grounding screws and clips are also available.

If fastening the box to a load center (electric service panel), slip the appropriate connector onto the cable, insert the cable through the knockout and connector, then tighten the connector to secure the cable to the box.

The Romex cable bare ground wire must be connected securely to a metal outlet box; Bakelite or other nonmetallic boxes are not permitted, simply because there's no connection to ground. Or else it must be secured to the green grounding screw on the receptacle or switch.

When running any kind of cable into a house, you should follow the approximate contour of the building and give reasonable protection against mechanical injury. If it is necessary to install it at right angles to something, you can run it through holes made in the framing or mount it on boards. You should not take shortcuts across free space.

Stripping and Connecting Wire

When stripping wire to connect it to terminal screws on receptacles and switches, use a wire stripper to cut off the insulation at a slight angle rather than square. You should remove about ¾" of it, then wrap the bare wire around the screw shank in a clockwise direction. In this way, when the screws are tightened, the wire will tend to tighten also; if they were counterclockwise, they could have a tendency to loosen.

For joining wires in electrical boxes, you should use solderless connectors, popularly known as wire nuts. These come in various sizes to accept various size wires. Tell the dealer what size wire you are using and he will give you the right size. Many brands come color coded, so that you can tell the gauge wire they're covering.

To join the wire, strip the insulation off each about ¾", then hold the wires together side by side—don't twist them—and stick them in the wire nut, turning the nut down over them. It will clamp them together tightly. Wrap electrical tape around the connections for extra security.

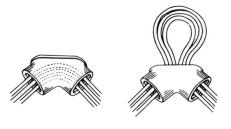

Many different types of fittings are used with conduit. Here elbow is used. It makes changing the wire direction much easier. Wires must be pulled through the conduit (which has been lubricated with compound) with a special puller.

Right and wrong way to trim insulation. It's best to use wire cutting tool.

Right way to connect wire to terminal screws

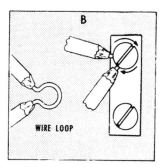

Another correct way to make a connection—always wrap wire end clockwise.

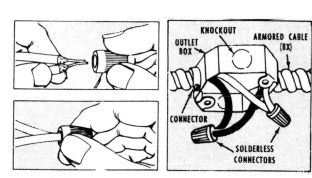

Better way to make connections is with wire nuts, also called solderless connectors.

Transformer for low-voltage wire

Scotch Lok Wire Nuts. They come in colors according to the gauge of wire they accept.

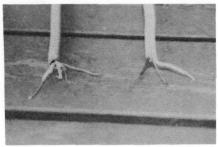

Left, BX (armored cable) and right, Romex (non-metallic cable). Standard Bx consists of two conductors and a bare bonding wire. Standard Romex also has two conductors and bare ground wire.

Cable carries information and has specs stamped on it. The stamp here means that the cable (Romex) is 14 gauge and has two conductors.

Occasionally you may have a need to splice wire. Here strip the wire back about ¾″, lay them together, and connect them with a wire nut. Or use a device called a crimping sleeve.

Low-Voltage Wiring

Low-voltage wire is any wire that can handle up to 90 volts. Its main advantage is that it doesn't carry enough current to shock. Hence, you can do things with it that you wouldn't do with normal wire.

For example, you can run it outside, instead of inside walls, thereby possibly saving a lot of mess and work. As such, it is commonly used to control outdoor lights. It is also used as bell wire. It comes in three gauges: 19, 20, and 22.

The power that flows through low-voltage wire comes from the same source as that which flows through other wiring: your electric service box. In its natural state the current would quickly burn up low-voltage wire; hence, a transformer is used to bring the voltage down to acceptable pressure. The transformer you buy depends on the item being wired. Its capacity must be matched to the wattage that the device draws.

Low-voltage wire is normally available only at an electrical supply house. Just describe the use to the dealer and he'll give you what you need.

Switches

A switch is nothing more than a device to either cut off or allow the flow of electrical current. There are many different types of switches, but the most commonly used are those designed for house wiring. Three switches occupy center stage: the single-pole, the three-way, and the four-way switch.

Single-Pole Switch

The single-pole switch is for controlling one light or group of lights from one point. You would be likely to find this type of switch in a room with only one entrance. As you enter the room, you flip the switch and the light goes on. As you leave it, you flip it off.

Single-pole switch. It has a screw on each side.

Three-Way Switches

This switch is handy when you want to control lights from two different locations. For example, on a stairs leading to a basement you'd have one three-way switch at the base of the stairs, one at the head. Another use would be one three-way switch at the head of a long corridor and one at the end. Or you might use it in a long kitchen with two entrances; one switch would be at one end, one at the other.

Four-Way Switches

This type of switch simply has more light-controlling capacity than the three-way: With it you are able to control separate lights from three or more different locations.

Single-pole, three-way, and four-way switches are commonly available with three kinds of *On-Off* action. The cheapest, and loudest is the snap action. You flip a toggle and the switch goes on with an audible (sometimes too audible) click. Another action is the quiet type. Here, the internal parts are constructed so that no sound is made when the switch is turned on or off.

Most expensive is the mercury switch. Here a tube of mercury in the switch tilts when you activate the handle to open or close the electrical contact. This switch is soundless. They are also the most expensive, but they are widely accepted as the most durable and literally should not wear out.

Also available are push-button types and rocker-type switches, which contain large molded sections that add a measure of decor. Many switches also come with illuminated handles, handy for spotting in a dark room. Replacement is done the same way as with a regular toggle switch.

Switches, like other electrical devices, are rated, usually to handle 10 or 15 amps. You can't use them with devices whose total current draw is greater than this.

BUYING TIPS

You can tell the difference between one switch and the other by the number of screws on each. A single-pole switch will have two brass colored screws.

A three-way switch will have three screws—two brass or silver, and the third dark, or copper colored. It may also have a green grounding screw.

A four-way switch will have four screws—two brass and two copper colored, or four brass colored and possibly another green screw.

Three-way switch. There will be another screw on the other side. A four-way switch would have two more screws.

Leviton calls this switch their "Decora" type. It has a quiet rocker-arm action.

Switch with illuminated toggle from Electracraft. It's handy for seeing in the dark.

Switch with plaster ears clipped off (it also comes this way). Switches and receptacles are screwed to boxes and wallplates are screwed to switches and receptacles.

Switches may also be obtained in duplex form.

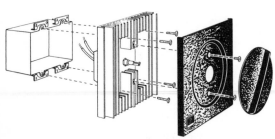

Fluorescent dimmer switch.

The location of the screws on the switches may be on one side of the switch or on both sides, depending on the manufacturer.

Depending on the installation situation, the location of the screws can make the attaching of wire easier.

Switches come in two grades, regular and "spec" (for specification). While both switches may be listed by UL as safe, the spec grade is more durable—it can take more abuse than the regular. The word *spec* will be imprinted on the switch, as well the amperage (the vast majority are 15 amps, but there are some 20-amp switches that are sometimes used in basements where high-wattage devices are used) and voltage.

INSTALLATION TIPS

Replacing a switch merely involves turning off the current at the fuse box or circuit breaker panel that controls the switch, noting the number of screws to identify the switch, and then reading the amperage and voltage and getting one of the same capacity and type. Or you can simply bring the old switch in and get a replacement. The wires should be hooked up the same way as the old switch—black to copper, silver to brass, and so forth. If you wish, you can make a note of where each goes so that you can be doubly sure of its location. Some people buy a replacement switch before they take out the old one. Then as each wire is unhooked from the old switch, they can attach it to the new. This reduces the chance of a mix-up.

Switches (and receptacles) also come with plaster ears. If the box is flush with the wall these ears can be clipped off and the switch screwed to the box. If the box is recessed too much, leave the ears on and let them overlap the opening in the wall. If the box is flush with the wall but you are adding paneling the ears should be left on to keep the switch flush with the paneling.

Dimmer Switch

Single-pole and three-way switches are also available in dimmer types. Here you are able, by manipulating a knob or toggle, to dim the lights to any degree you wish. Aside from the ambience this can lend, you will also save on electrical bills because the more you dim the lights, the less wattage you will use.

A dimmer switch for incandescent lights is constructed just like a regular one and can be replaced the same way.

Dimmer switches are also available for fluorescent lights, but these are far too large to be mounted in a normal switch box. Indeed, the dimmer switch may be 6″ to 8″ wide—three times the size of a normal switch. Most companies who make this item sell the dimmer, box, and cover as one unit.

Dimmer switches are commonly available to handle lights that total 300 to 600 watts, but large sizes (1,000- and 2,000-watt units) are also available.

House-Wiring Switches

A variety of other switches are available for house wiring.

Combination switch. In the combination switch, one part is a switch, the other a receptacle. These are most commonly available with quiet and silent switch actions.

Pilot-light switch. A particularly useful switch is one with a pilot light. This is simply a switch with a pilot light that stays on when a particular piece of equipment is operating. For example, you may have a fan in the attic and don't want to climb up there to see if it is on. If the pilot light is on, you'll know the fan is operating.

Miniaturized switch. If you have a small space to work in, there are miniaturized switches (also known as interchangeable switches; Despard is one brand name). Indeed, you can fit three of these switches into the space required by a normal-size switch. These switches require a mounting strap. The strap has three openings in it to put in switches, receptacles, or a combination of the two; a screwdriver is used to push against a pressure point on the strap, and the switch is locked in place. The strap has two screw holes for normal mounting to the box.

You might use a miniature switch or receptacle where wiring is adequate and you want the convenience of two switches or outlets where you'd only normally have one because of lack of space.

Nontamperable switch. Occasionally, one has use for a switch that must not be able to be turned off accidentally. Here the key-type switch is good. In construction it is just like a standard switch, except that it must be turned on and off with a key. This type of switch is only used on machines and is good where children are present.

Timer switch. Switches (and receptacles) also come with built-in timers. Models that will automatically activate—turn on—every one hour or every two hours are commonly available. This type of switch might be useful for home security, to turn on lights at specified times. (For more information on timers, see page 139.) It is installed exactly like a regular switch.

Switch with pilot light

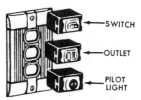

Despard switch. Three switches could be used in it. It's a good device when wall space is limited.

Switch that can only be turned on by a key. It comes with the key.

Outside and safety switches. Switches used on the exterior of the home are made the same way and in the same sizes and styles as those inside. The only difference is that they are housed in weatherproof boxes and covers.

Other common safety switches are for use with heavy equipment, such as a pump for a pool or an oil burner. These come with or without a separate fuse. For safety, the fuse can be removed, making the switch inactive.

Non-House-Wiring Switches

The switches thus far discussed are all designed to be installed in the walls of the house. There are other switches that are designed to be installed on the electrical cords of lamps, appliances, and the like.

Cord switch. The cord switch, for example, is designed to be installed along the length of an electrical lamp cord. It is commonly used for convenience. You can turn off the lamp from a remote position, such as from bed or a comfortable arm chair. You may purchase the cord switch in the form of either a regular switch or a dimmer.

Here, as with any kind of switch, one must match the device to the capacity of the device that it will be installed on. Switches for lamp cords (regular and dimmer) are rated at 300 watts.

One type, designed for this (Gem is one manufacturer) comes in halves that are screwed together. The halves are unscrewed and the wire connected inside. No splicing of the wire is required. Heavier cord switches must be spliced in place.

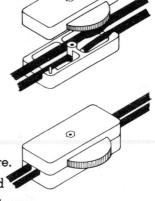

1. split wire, cut one only.

2. place wire in half without wheel.

3. press halves together. note that points pierce insulation to make contact with copper inside cut wire.

4. replace nut into switch and tighten screw until secure.

Cord switch from Gem Electric showing wiring diagram provided by the company.

Canopy switch. This switch is also available for table and floor use on lamp cord. It comes with wires stripped at the ends ready for attaching. The action is push-button.

Rotary switch. The rotary switch (which gets its name from the fact that the button is rotated to activate it) is available for a variety of purposes. You can get them to control table and floor lamps, small appliances, and for controlling two individual or built-in units in an appliance or for controlling two circuits. Twisting the switch to a certain point produces various levels of light. Rotary switches come with stripped leads, which are spliced to existing wire.

Toggle switch. This switch is also available for use on table and floor lamps and small appliances. Heavy-duty toggle switches have a capacity to handle large portable tools, vacuum cleaners, and motors. There are single-throw types, where the action is *On-Off,* and double-throw, where the action is *On-Off-On.*

Other switches. Two other types of switches are the push-button fluorescent starter switch and the push-button momentary-*On* switch. The first switch eliminates the need for a separate starter in a fluorescent light. The other switch is for use on portable tools and motors. Both are available in from 15 to 40 watts. Another type of push switch is for lamps, fixtures, and small appliances.

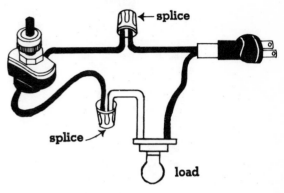

Canopy switch for control of table and floor lamps or appliance.

Push switch from Gem is for lamps, small appliances, and fixtures.

Dimmer cord switch. It can be spliced onto a lamp cord.

Switch for surface wiring

Receptacles

Receptacles, also called outlets, are devices intended for tapping off power where needed in the house. They are available in single or duplex (two outlets in one device). Like switches, they have terminal screws. The line, or hot side, screw is copper or brass colored, the neutral or negative side is silver. Receptacles may also have a green grounding screw on one corner of the frame. To this the bare ground wire on the cable may be attached.

Standard duplex receptacle with plaster ears, which enables receptacle to be mounted flush in hole in the wall when box is recessed too much.

Single receptacle

Like switches, receptacles are rated in terms of amperage and voltage capacity, and the device plugged into it must not exceed this capacity (this will be stamped on the device; if it comes in a package, it will be there). The normal rating for lighting-circuit receptacles is 15 amps and 125 volts. For large appliances, switches with 30-amp, 250-volt ratings are used. It should be noted that a receptacle may be used for smaller amperages and voltages than its rating. For example, the 250-volt receptacle can be used for 220-volt appliance, 240, and so on up to 250 volts. If the rating were exceeded—if say, a refrigerator were plugged into a 15-amp, 125-volt receptacle, the receptacle and the wires would burn up. Receptacles usually have far more capacity then needed. The average lamp draws 3 amps, while the receptacle is 15.

Like switches, receptacles may be wired by looping the bared ends of the wires onto the terminal screws on the side of the device or by pushing the bared ends into clamp holes in the back. The holes are color coded to indicate which wire goes where. Electricians use the latter device because it is faster than the screw-terminal type, but there is wide agreement that attaching wires to screws is more secure.

Almost all receptacles today have one U-shaped and two vertical grounding slots. All receptacles are—or should be—grounded. One type is automatically grounded when it is attached to the box. On other types a wire must be fastened from the screws to the box.

Receptacles are also available for dryers, air-conditioners, water pumps, and other heavy-use equipment. Here the am-

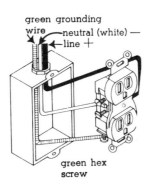

Receptacle showing green ground screw.

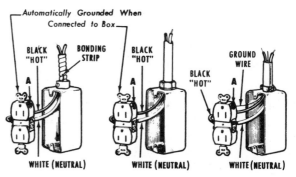

Ways receptacles are grounded. *Left,* box has metal strap that, when connected to metal box, is grounded, because metal box is connected to armor on BX cable. *Center,* box is similarly connected, but to metal conduit. *Right,* box has separate ground wire. A receptacle must have three slots—two straight and a U-shaped one—or it can't be grounded.

Receptacles also come with switches.　　　Range receptacle

perage may be as high as 50. Again, to get the proper size replacement receptacle, look for the rating stamped on the device.

Changing a Two-Wire Plug to a Grounded System

Prior to 1976 the National Electrical Code did not require a grounded system anywhere except on appliances in kitchens and bathrooms. The reason this rule was inadequate is that leaking current will electrify its metal appliance housing if it has no path to the ground. An appliance is simply unsafe without grounding. Pigtail adapters are designed to convert from two-wire to three-wire plugs. The appliance is plugged into the adapter, which has three holes; then the adapter is plugged into the receptacle, with the pigtail secured to the wall plate screw. Better and safer is an adapter that has a small strap on top through which the wall plate screw is run. In any case, the wiring system itself must be grounded, or the adapter is meaningless.

BUYING TIPS

Like switches, receptacles are made in spec grade. You can buy outlets and switches in bulk and save some money. Switches are commonly available ten to the box, while receptacles come twenty to the box.

Multiple-Outlet Strip

The average home does not have all its receptacles located in the right places, or enough of them. Where you need the

Multiple-outlet strip is a good way to get neat convenience outlets. Strip is spliced to the existing circuit, but the circuit must be evaluated to make sure not too much current will be drawn.

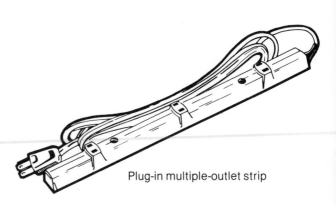

Plug-in multiple-outlet strip

These plug-in devices are usually not a good idea. They can overload a circuit because people who use them don't think about what kind of current is being drawn.

convenience of a number of receptacles, for example, over a workbench or the kitchen counter, consider purchasing what is commonly called a multiple-outlet strip. This is basically a strip of receptacles constructed primarily of metal or plastic.

The strips come prewired in five or six different lengths and with the outlets 6″, 12″, and 18″ apart. They come in two- and three-wire types. To install, a plate is mounted on the wall and two or three wires from an electrical box linked to the strip. The cover is then screwed back on. The metallic type will take more abuse than the plastic type. Before using this type of device, you should calculate what you are going to plug into it to make sure that the circuit can carry the load and will not be overloaded.

Ground Fault Circuit Interrupters

This device is a relative newcomer to the electrical scene. If you are using a supposedly grounded device and there is just a minimal leakage of electricity, the GFI will sense it and shut off the current before a circuit breaker or fuse will.

Ground fault circuit interrupters are available for installation in either the circuit breaker panel, in the wall as an outlet, or as a portable device.

The GFI may be installed in the place of any standard circuit breaker as long as it has the same size and current capacity. Installation is as simple as a new breaker. The GFI acts as a circuit breaker—that is, it will stop current flow in case of an overload on the line—but it will also cut the circuit off if the electrical leakage is small.

This can be an inconvenience on house circuits, because normally there is a certain amount of leakage. You'll be running to the circuit breaker panel all day to turn the device back on. Most people, therefore, opt for installing the GFI only where it will control circuits that run into the kitchen, bath, and pool area, where there is water present and therefore greater electrical hazard. The National Electrical Code requires them in new work in kitchens and baths.

Ground fault circuit interrupter.

Receptacle Breakers.

There are a couple of kinds of these. They come in a standard duplex receptacle and are installed in a standard wall box.

One type of GFI here controls only one outlet. The user is protected when he plugs anything into that particular outlet. If it trips, GFI can be instantly reset; no trip to the circuit breaker panel is required. The device is not affected by current that comes to it from the service panel; it only controls current going to the device.

Another type of GFI can protect more than one outlet. With proper wiring it can protect other outlets beyond the one protected.

Finally, there are portable devices for use with portable power equipment outdoors. These plug into a grounded outlet and provide the same protection as other GFI's.

This is a safety device. It plugs into a receptacle, keeping it covered when not in use. Good for children's rooms or where pets are.

Timers

It may become desirable at certain times to have the lights go on and off automatically, such as when you are away or for convenience. There are a variety of timers available.

Simple plug-in timers can be attached to any kind of lamp. A time clock is installed in the circuit of the lights to be controlled and is connected to a switch. When you throw the switch, the timer takes over the circuit, turning the lights on and off depending on how the clock is set.

Timers come in a variety of sizes, but 1,000-watt units are common. These can handle lights that use up to 1,000 watts.

A more sophisticated timer can be used to control the lights from anywhere in the house. This is commonly installed in the bedroom so that you can turn the lights off or on without getting out of bed.

One other timer is basically a switch that can be installed beside a back door and that controls outside lights. It can be used to turn them off at dusk and then on in the morning.

Plugs, Cords, and Sockets

Plugs

Appliances, lamps, and other electrical items occasionally require plug replacement. There are two types available: the male and female. The male plugs have prongs, while the female plugs have slots to accept them.

The male plugs come with either two or three prongs (two straight and one U-shaped prong for grounding). Plug housings are made of metal, plastic, ceramic, rubber, or nylon. Many electricians prefer nylon.

Some replacement plugs come with a screw-clamp device that compresses the neck of the plug, thereby gripping the cord so that it won't disconnect from the plug. This is a desirable feature simply because plugs are commonly pulled from the receptacle by the cord, and repeated jerkings will put stress where the wires are connected to the plug. Also, the clamp screw eliminates the necessity of attaching the cord to the plug with an Underwriters' knot, which is difficult to tie because of the limited room inside the plug housing.

Plugs, like other electrical items, are rated to handle the current of the particular device. This will appear on the name plate and be in terms of amperage, usually where the wires disappear into the housing of the device. Just get one to match. For example, the plug on an extension cord is almost always 15 amps and a three-wire type. Replacement plugs for appliance cords may be 20, 30, or 50 amps. Dryer plugs may be 30 amps and range up to 50 amps.

Clamp-type plug. Note screws on the neck for tightening cord in place.

Standard plugs are either the open-construction or the dead-front type. In the open-construction type, there are screw terminals covered by an insulating disc that can be pried up and slipped off the prongs. The wires are then looped around the screw shanks and the screws tightened. On appliances either there are two screws—copper and nickel, if the cord is two-wire—or there is an additional green grounding screw if a third wire is used.

The open-construction type is being phased out. Since January 1978 Underwriters' Laboratories are only listing plugs with dead fronts, though open-construction supplies will continue to be sold until they are depleted.

The dead-front type is a safer plug. Here the wires are buried in the plug. To reach them, you must remove screws recessed in the front of the plug and take off a thick cap. The stripped wires are either mounted in pressure slots or secured to screws. This type of plug costs more than the open-construction type.

Appliance plugs. A number of plugs for appliances, such as griddles, are female. They plug into the male prongs on the device. Such plugs can be separated into two halves by removing the screw or screws securing them.

Clamp plugs for lamps. The plugs just discussed are all connected to terminal screws. One other type, which eliminates the job of stripping wire for attaching it to the terminal screws, is available for lamp wire (no. 18) cords. Typically, the bad plug and about an inch or so of wire is cut off. A detachable piece holding the prongs is pulled out of the plug. The prongs are spread wide apart, and the end of the cord is slipped into a slot in the detachable piece. The prongs are then squeezed together. Inside, tiny teeth pierce the cord, making electrical contact. The piece is snapped back into the shell. The plug is ready to be used. Another variation: The cord end is slipped into a hole in the plug, then is pulled. As it is, it clamps in place and electrical contact is made.

to assemble:

1. strip wire ½" remove front cover from plug. feed wire through cord hole. tie underwriters' knot in wire.
2. pull wire back through plug until stopped by knot.
3. wrap wire ends clockwise around terminal screws and tighten screws.
4. replace cover.

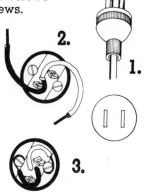
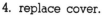

Open-construction plug with instructions for wiring. An Underwriter's knot is tied to relieve strain on the cord.

This type of plug converts a two-wire outlet to three-wire.

Range and dryer plug

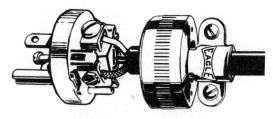

Dead-front plug, shown open

This is for a lamp cord. It is connected to the cord without stripping wires.

Appliance cord set. Spotted cord identifies this as asbestos insulated.

Cords

You can get any kind of cord in any length you wish, to replace either lamp or appliance cord. Again, get the capacity required by the device, and the type.

Items such as roasters and grills require heat-resistant cord, such as asbestos. The easiest way to do this is simply to ask for the cord in terms of end use. If you ask at an electrical supply house for a cord for a toaster, you'll get it.

You can also buy cord sets—plug, cord, and terminals or bare-wire leads for attaching to the device. You could also, of course, make your own cord set. However, in the higher amperages the cord is only available in round black rubber, and you may consider this unsightly on certain appliances. If you have any difficulty getting the exact cord you want at an electrical supply store, then try a store that sells appliance parts.

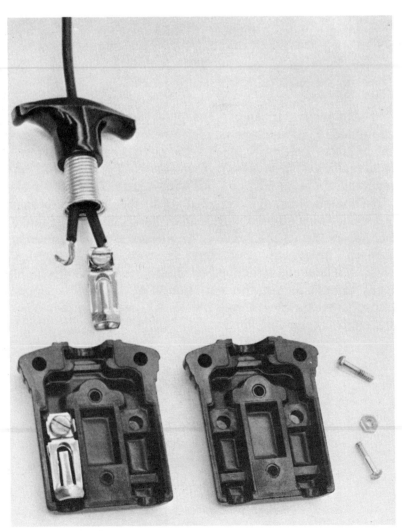

Female section of cord set showing the connections inside

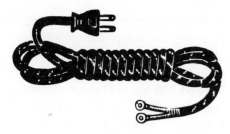

This type of appliance cord attaches to terminals inside the appliance.

Plugs on appliances may also be replaced. They come in different sizes.

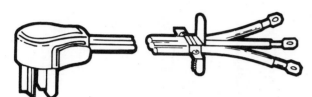 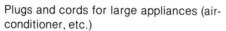

Plugs and cords for large appliances (air-conditioner, etc.)

Extension cords. When you don't have a receptacle installed in the right place, an extension cord may be used. These come in two- and three-wire types, but today almost all are three-wire dead-front. It is always desirable to use the grounded one (this assumes, of course, that your house system is grounded).

Extension cords are available in lengths of from 6' to 100'. Again, match the amperage draw of the device to the cord used. Cords are available to resist oil and acid. If you intend to get the cord for a mower, hedge clipper, or other powered cutting device, always buy a cord that is safety yellow or orange. A black one can be virtually invisible and can get cut accidentally.

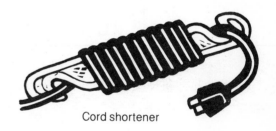

Cord shortener

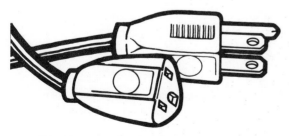

Female and male plugs on extension cord

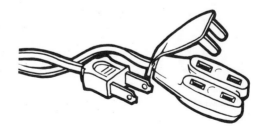

Extension cord with safety cap

143

Three-way socket

Sockets

You may buy either a complete lamp socket or just the mechanism. Both are available. Some sockets are for two-way lights—simple *On* and *Off* action—while others are to provide three levels of light—30, 70, and 100 watt. These are called two-filament sockets. In any case, though, the wiring is the same. There are two screws, one copper, one nickel, with a bared wire looped under each. It doesn't matter which wire goes to which cord screw. Sockets to convert a regular socket to a dimmer type are also available.

Pull-chain socket. It has simple *On-Off* action.

Used to replace interior mechanisms.

Interior mechanisms are available for replacing in sockets.

Bulb fits in this socket. Device is surface mounted.

Socket reducer. This can be screwed into a regular socket when you want to mount a smaller bulb.

Current tap. It can be plugged into a lamp socket for a handy power outlet

shell

interior

Socket used to change regular socket with dimmer. It is wired the same way.

cap
set screw

threaded
nipple
on lamp

Wall Plates

Wall plates for switches and receptacles are made either of metal or of nonmetallic material, such as Bakelite. Normally, the plates are either white, brown, brass, or aluminum colored, but there are a great number of decorator plates—wood grain, bright colors, and designs, so you can get a style to suit your home.

Standard white or brown wall plates can be bought singly or in lots of twenty-five, but the average do-it-yourselfer would not need this many. Decorator plates are sold singly.

Just as there are single and duplex outlets, wall plates can be matched to the device at hand. Multigang plates (more than one receptacle or switch is covered) are also available. You can get them to handle up to half a dozen switches and receptacles if you wish.

Wall plates come in a tremendous array of styles. Shown is one manufacturer's display.

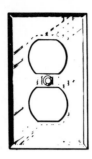

Standard duplex receptacle plate. Plates come with screws.

Standard switch plate. Plates are beveled so that they cover switches and receptacles, which protrude slightly from the wall.

Wall plates come with the screws for installing them. Installation is very simple. You just place the plate over the receptacle or switch, then run the screw or screws through into corresponding threads on the switch or receptacle.

Wall plates are also available in a jumbo size. These can come in handy if you accidentally overcut the opening in the wall when you install a switch or receptacle: The oversized plate will hide the damage.

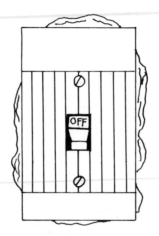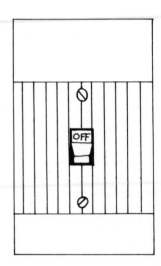

Oversized plates of various types are available. If you overcut an opening, a jumbo plate will cover it.

Light Fixtures and Bulbs

There are fixtures for both the inside and the outside of the home, and they can differ greatly in style, shape, and color. Indeed, there are entire stores devoted to light fixtures. Following, though, is a capsule roundup of the kinds available.

Ceiling Fixtures

These, of course, are mounted in the ceiling. They usually come with three wires. Mounting is in an appropriately shaped and sized electrical box. It usually can be done in one of two different ways: Either there will be an existing threaded stud or there will not. If there is a stud, the fixture can be screwed in place with a device called a hickey. If there is no stud, then a crossbar hanger must be used. Other hardware is available for particular situations. Electrical supply stores commonly carry a variety which can be tailored to your needs.

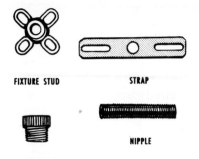

FIXTURE STUD   STRAP

NIPPLE

EXTENSION NIPPLE

Typical hardware for hanging fixtures. In most cases hanging fixtures is a "Rube Goldberg" arrangement: You combine various pieces of hardware to hang particular fixtures.

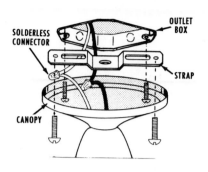

The ceiling fixture here is screwed to a strap, which is screwed to the outlet box.

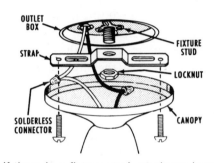

If there is a fixture stud, as shown here, the strap may be screwed to the stud, then the fixture screwed to the strap.

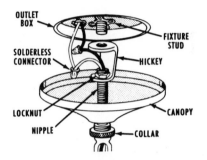

In the case of a deep fixture, a hickey or coupling is screwed to the fixture stud; locknut and nipple are also utilized.

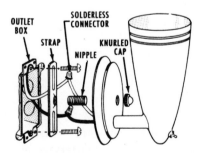

To hang the wall fixture here, a strap is secured to the outlet box; then a knurled cap is screwed on the nipple and the nipple screwed to the strap.

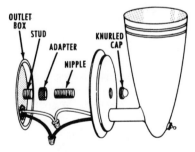

Arrangement when there is a fixture stud

You should make sure, when hanging a ceiling fixture, that the support is strong enough. Some fixtures can weigh as much as 60 or 70 pounds and will come down if not properly mounted.

Wiring connections may be a puzzle because you may not be able to know which wire is hot—the black or the red; one will be the switch wire. To find out, test. Connect white to white and black to black. If this doesn't work, connect white to white and black to red; that should work.

Porcelain Fixtures

The old-fashioned porcelain or Bakelite ceiling fixtures are still commonly available. They may come with a socket for a bulb or a socket and outlet; the latter can be handy for plugging in a power tool or perhaps for a trouble light.

Porcelain fixtures are generally available in sizes ranging from 250 to 600 watts. By all means get the largest capacity that the house circuit will allow. For the slight extra cost it will be well worth it.

Three kinds of old-fashioned porcelain fixtures: *left,* with pull chain; *center,* with receptacle for plugging into; *right,* keyless. Some types (not shown) come with lead wires. These are the easiest to use. All these fit into boxes of either 3¼″ or 4″ diameter.

INSTALLATION TIPS

Porcelain fixtures come either with screw terminals, or prewired with leads, or with two leads—white and black lead wires ready for connecting. The lead type is the easiest to install. Fixture sizes may be 3″, 4″, 5¼″, and, of course, a box it can fit into must be bought if you are installing a new one.

Since you will likely be working in a garage or damp area when installing a porcelain fixture, stand on a board for safety while doing it.

If required, the sockets on porcelain fixtures can be replaced—you needn't buy a complete new fixture.

Other Fixtures

Other fixtures include chandeliers and hanging lamps; that is, ones that hang off a chain, itself looped on a fancy toggle bolt set into the ceiling. This type of lamp can save you the job of putting in a receptacle if you need light in an area where a receptacle isn't located.

Outdoor Fixtures. There are many different kinds of fixtures for outdoor use. Most of them are simple to install. They have ½″ pipe threads for screwing into boxes and are set into the box. Other fixtures, a canopy type, screw into the box but cover it. These are mainly for decoration.

Outdoor light fixtures

Bulbs

There are two main kinds of bulbs for the home—fluorescent and incandescent. For energy saving, and for saving money, the fluorescent is by far the better buy. The same light can be produced for 30 watts that it takes a 40 watt-incandescent to achieve.

Fluorescent lamps. This is how they're known in the trade, and they come in many different sizes and types. For home use, however, there are three types you might want to consider: soft white, warm white, and daylight.

The soft-white tube gives a cool, even light and is the best for pure lighting. The warm white does not give nearly as much good light and is primarily for decoration and ambience. The daylight fluorescent gives a very bright light that most people dislike.

Tip: If something goes wrong with a fluorescent tube, the starter is often at fault.

If something is wrong with a fluorescent light, the starter is often at fault. It can be removed by pressing it in and twisting it in the direction indicated by the word *Remove* on the device. Get the same size starter from your dealer.

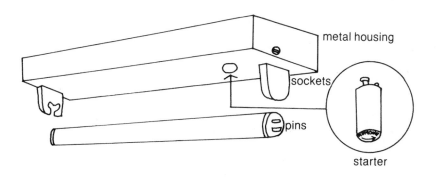

Incandescent bulbs. These are generally available in wattages up to 200. A problem many people have today is with incandescent bulbs burning out. This often occurs when one's home is located near a transformer of the utility company. For this problem, try 130-volt bulbs. Voltage from the utility company varies. If it goes up to 128, and your bulb is only 120, it will burn out. The 130-volt bulb won't.

A great many other kinds of bulbs are available. Spotlights, low-voltage bulbs, colored bulbs (one company, Yorkville Industries, devotes all of a thick, handsome catalogue to bulbs). The only advice here is to visit local outlets and look over what is available.

Lamp Parts

In recent years there has been a surge in the interest people have in making their own lamps. Consequently, there are more parts available as well as complete carded kits that provide all the hardware for making a lamp, except for the lamp body, which can be created by drilling a hole into a bottle or some other container.

Following is a roundup of the main lamp parts. Various outlets carry them, including electrical supply stores, discount houses, and hardware stores.

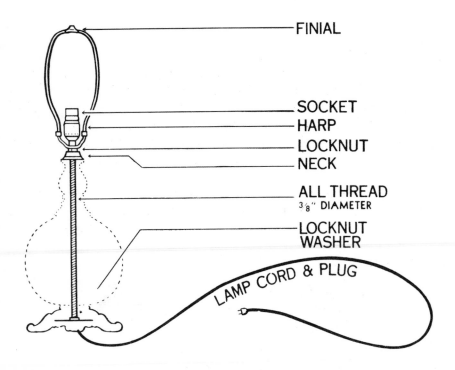

FINIAL

SOCKET
HARP
LOCKNUT
NECK

ALL THREAD
3/8" DIAMETER
LOCKNUT
WASHER

LAMP CORD & PLUG

Threaded Rods

The spine of a lamp is a piece of hollow threaded rod that runs from the base of the body, where it is secured by a locknut, through the top, where it is also secured by a locknut and a couple of other pieces of hardware.

Commonly, threaded rod is available in ⅛″ IPS, which means, like plumbing pipe, that the internal diameter is ⅛″. The entire rod is ⅜″ wide. The wire, of course, runs through the rod. Other sizes of threaded rod are available, but ⅛″ is standard. It is commonly available in brass finish and in steel.

Locknuts and washers are also available in various sizes, but the great majority are designed to fit the ⅛″ IPS rod. Locknuts are normally decorative—brass finished—because they are exposed to view.

Wire

Standard lamp cord size is no. 18–2 SPT-1. It is commonly called zip cord because of the ease with which you can split the wire (it is solid thermoplastic with a groove down the center) when stripping insulation for attaching to the socket. Cord can be bought either without a plug or in set lengths with the plug attached. Underwriters' Laboratory suggests that the cord used on a lamp be no longer than 9′.

Harps

A harp has a hole at the bottom. It slips over the top of the threaded rod and is secured by a locknut. The socket is screwed in place over this. The top of the harp is then slipped over the threaded rod and secured by a decorative cap called a finial. Finials are available in a wide variety of styles. The wire goes through the rod and is screwed to the socket.

Harps are available in a wide variety of sizes up to around 2′ high.

To remove a harp, two retaining sleeves at the bottom of the legs of the harp must be lifted; the harp is then squeezed together and lifts out.

Threaded rod comes in a variety of lengths for lamp making. It is normally ⅛″, inside diameter.

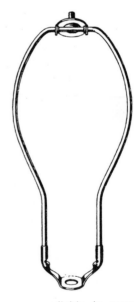

Harps are available in many different sizes. They change the shape of the lamp.

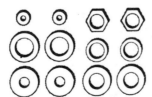

Locknuts are used to hold the threaded rod to the lamp at the top and bottom.

Finials are screwed onto the top of lamps. They are also available in many different sizes.

Sockets

A variety of sockets is used on lamps. Some have simple *On-Off* action. Others have a turnbutton that can provide three levels of light. Most sockets have a setscrew that keeps them stationary when you install a light, but inside they are essentially the same. There are two terminal screws: Wires stripped of insulation are wrapped around the screws in a clockwise direction, and the screws are tightened. It doesn't matter which wire goes to which screw.

Other Lamp Parts

In addition to the basic parts just discussed, there are a few other items that can add to lamp-making capacity or serve as replacement parts. These come carded.

Couplings. These are used to join two lengths of rod.

Reducing bushings. These are used to reduce the inside diameter of the rod from ¼″ to ⅛″.

Clip adapters. These can be used when a lamp has no harp. They clip onto the bulb, and the shade goes over a projecting part on the top of the adapter.

Couplings are used to join lengths of rod.

Reducing bushings allow you to change from one size threaded rod to another.

If a lamp has no harp, a clip adapter is used. It clamps onto the bulb.

Building a Lamp

Building a lamp is a very worthwhile endeavor, considering most lamps' retail price. And it's easy. If you wish, you can buy a kit, but you may save even more by building it with separately bought component parts. Follow this procedure:

1. Slip a piece of threaded rod through the body of the lamp. Secure it to the base of the body with a locknut.

2. Add the lamp neck on the top of the rod.

3. Screw a brass locknut on top of the neck and tighten it with your fingers.

4. Make a mark ½″ above the locknut on the rod.

5. Take the lamp apart to cut the threaded rod with a hacksaw.

6. Cut off excess rod. To facilitate this, install a locknut on each side of your cutline. After cutting, slowly remove the locknuts from the cut ends. This dresses the ends. Remove any remaining burrs carefully with a file.

7. Reinstall the rod.

8. Slip the harp in place and secure it with the knurled nut.

9. Screw the socket cap in place; tighten the setscrew to hold it stationary.

10. Thread lamp cord through the lamp, allowing 6″ to 10″ of excess to pass out the top for convenience.

11. Strip ½″ of insulation off each wire with a razor. Wrap the bare wire around each screw in a clockwise direction, then turn the screws down tight.

12. Draw the wire through from the base; this draws the socket down toward the cap. Snap the socket into the socket cap.

13. Mount the plug (for further information, see pages 140–144). A clamp-on type is convenient.

14. Slip the harp in place. Put on the shade and secure it with a finial at the top, then add the bulb.

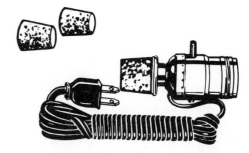

A number of companies, such as Electra Craft, sell lamp kits—socket, cord, and corks for plugging a bottle at top and bottom if necessary.

Repairing a Lamp

Repairing a lamp should be easy once you know how it is constructed.

If the plug goes bad, you can replace it with a clamp-on device. If the socket is bad, it is a simple matter to replace it with a new one. And if the wire is bad, a replacement can also be attached with little difficulty.

IV

PLUMBING
HARDWARE

How a Plumbing System Works

A residential plumbing system is actually three systems: the fresh or potable water supply, the drainage system, and the fixtures and appliances.

Water System

There are three possible sources of water: either a municipal water works, a spring, or a well.

Water that starts its journey to your house in a water works is purified there, then travels through a series of pipes until it enters a single main service line, usually ¾″ in diameter, into your house. As it enters, it goes through a meter, which records its use. From there it branches out into a pair of narrow (usually ½″) diameter pipes that travel side by side throughout the house and terminate at either appliances or fixtures that use the water. One of the lines is for cold water and one is for hot. The water becomes hot by being routed through the hot water heater before it begins its journey through the house.

All fresh water travels under pressure, which is the reason it gushes out when, for example, you turn on a faucet.

Different names have been given to the water pipes. Those that travel vertically at least one floor are called risers. Lines that travel horizontally to fixtures and appliances are called branch lines.

Valves. At various points on the pipes there are valves, which are faucetlike devices for shutting down water supply to the pipes when repair is needed. These are on runs to control specific lengths and are usually (or should be) under sinks and toilets: a hot and cold water one for the sink, and one for the toilet tank.

Valves are also located at the bottoms of risers; these are for when you want to drain the pipes. Additionally, homes also usually have one or two valves at the water meter. One is called the meter shutoff and is on the street side of the meter; the other is on the house side and is called the main shutoff. Turning either of these valves will stop all water flow to the house. It is good practice to shut off the main valve as a safety precaution whenever you want to shut the water off.

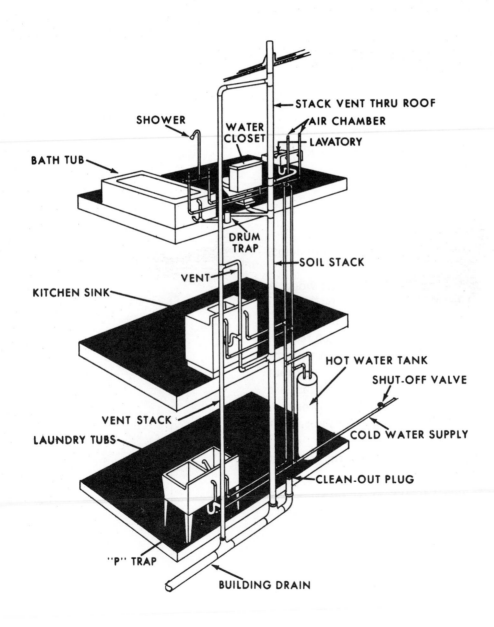

Air chambers. Every plumbing system also has—or should have (not all systems have them)—air chambers. These are vertical pieces of capped pipe that jut up from water supply pipes at the point where the pipe enters the fixture. In essence, an air chamber is a shock absorber. When the pipes are handling excess water, the excess enters the air chambers; otherwise, the pipes could start vibrating, a malady called water hammer, and possibly rupture from the shock.

Fixtures. There are three kinds of fixtures in the house: sink, tub, and toilet, and these are the main devices where water is used. Outside faucets, also known as sillcocks, may also be considered fixtures, but they are called fittings.

The Drainage System

The other part of a plumbing system is the drainage system, technically known as DWV system to describe what it does: drains away wastes at the same time as it vents them. In simplest terms, the DWV system is composed of waste pipes, a soil stack, traps, and vents.

The function of these things can be seen in the way a sink works. Waste runs out of the sink to a series of pipes that lead to the waste pipes, usually pipes with a diameter of 1½" or 2", which are sloped and run to the soil stack. The stack is a large pipe—usually 3" or 4" in diameter—that runs from the lowest point in the house to the highest and emerges about 6" through the roof. In older homes cast iron was commonly used, whereas in newer homes copper and plastic are used. From the stack the waste goes to the building drain, a horizontal pipe that runs across the house and leads to the sewer line and to the disposal system—sewer, septic tank, or cesspool.

Pipes that go from the toilets to the stack are called soil pipes. There are no branch lines here. The soil pipe drains into the soil stack directly. Drain lines only carry sink waste, soil pipes only carry toilet waste. The entire system operates by gravity.

Traps. The traps are safety devices. They are shaped to trap water, and thus they're constantly filled with water so that gases and vermin can't back up into the house through drain holes. Sink traps are separate pieces of tubing, whereas toilets are shaped to trap water: There are also drum traps for tubs and a trap and fresh air inlet where the soil pipe leaves the building.

Vents. Venting is required to release gases, but there is another important reason: It keeps the air pressure in the system equalized. Water from the drain or waste lines can't back up by a siphoning action into the fresh water system.

All fixtures, as mentioned, are connected to the soil stack. However, if the distance between fixture and stack is too long, there may be one or more other stacks. These also will be vented. In essence, a stack has two purposes: as waste line and vent line. It's a waste line below the fixture, a vent line above.

Cleanout plugs are located at the bottom of each soil stack and wherever the waste pipe changes direction, because that's where blockages often occur. These plugs can be removed and a cleanout tool (snake) inserted for clearing the blockage.

Pipe and Fittings

Pipe for plumbing—either water or waste pipe—is always referred to by its inside diameter. A 1″ pipe, then, has a 1″ inside diameter; its actual diameter will be greater, depending on the thickness of the particular material. When pipe is referred to here, it is always in terms of its inside diameter.

All pipe is male. That is, it is designed to fit into fittings, which are always female. Understanding this concept can lead to a quicker understanding of many other plumbing parts, which also are described in male-female designations.

Waste Pipe

Though there is a variety of kinds of waste pipe available, the use of some has faded, while others have come to the forefront. Since local plumbing codes may still allow less popular material, however, all common types are discussed.

Galvanized pipe. Galvanized steel pipe is not nearly so prevalent as it once was. One reason is that it must be threaded to be attached to fittings. A plumber can use an electrical vise to do this (or a plumbing supply store may do it), but it is still time-consuming, and in certain situations (say you are replacing a fitting) it must be threaded in place, a difficult job. Also, it has a tendency to scale with certain kinds of water, which leads to blockages.

For waste pipe, the 1½″, 2″, and 3″ sizes are used. It comes 21′ long, but plumbing supply stores commonly cut it to the size desired and thread it.

Cast-iron pipe. This is still very popular for waste pipe; indeed, its popularity has increased because of the new ways available for joining it. The pipe may be used above or below ground.

Cast-iron pipe may come with one end plain, or straight, and the other bell shaped; this is known as the spigot end. The old way of joining pieces is to insert the plain end into the bell end, then seal with lead and oakum. This is a time-consuming process and not without danger: If water is introduced to the hot lead, an explosion can result.

Newer cast-iron pipe is hubless—both ends are plain—and this permits much easier joining. Here the cut ends are slipped into a neoprene gasket, which is secured, in turn, with stainless steel clamps. These are tightened with a special wrench (which you can rent) to a torque of 48 pounds. The wrench is designed to slip after the desired torque is reached; in other words, you can't overtighten.

Fittings for cast iron are also joined with neoprene gaskets and clamps. The easiest way to cut cast iron pipe is with a snap cutter, which you can rent.

While this is a good method of joining, the resulting joints are flexible and the pipe will require more solid support so that it doesn't bend so much that the connection pulls apart. Indeed, it is not yet known how hubless pipe is performing in the ground because it is too new a product.

Cast-iron pipe is commonly available in length of 5′ and 10′ and in diameters of 2″, 3″, and 4″ for home use. Clamps and gaskets are also available.

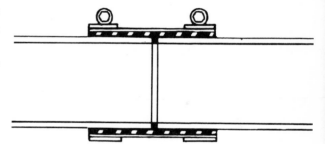

A new way of joining cast-iron pipe is with a neoprene gasket and clamps.

Clay pipe. Vitrified clay pipe or glazed pipe is also used for waste lines. It is commonly used underground, where its ability to resist acid makes it a good choice. It is much less popular today than it once was. The soil under this pipe must be firm, or the pipe can bend and break. Or else it must be supported by boards solidly set in the ground.

Copper tube. Copper pipe for waste is called DWV tube. It is rigid and is available in lengths of 10′ and 20′ and in various diameters. For the home the 3″ size is commonly used for the connection to the water closet.

Copper tube is expensive. There are many different fittings for joining it, and while there is a variety of ways to do it, the most commonly used is sweating, or soldering. This is quite easy to do once you get the hang of it. The key is cleanliness. When the pipe is cleaned and properly heated and fluxed, the solder is sucked into the joint quite readily.

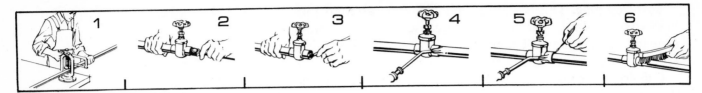

Sweating (soldering) copper tubing to fittings as shown in sequence from NIBCO Inc.

1 Cut tube end square. Ream, burr, and size.

2 Use a sand cloth or steel wire brush to clean both tube and cup to a bright metal. Steel wool is not recommended.

3 Apply flux to outside of tube and inside of solder cup. Surfaces to be joined must be completely covered. Use flux sparingly.

4 Be sure that the valve is fully open. Apply heat to the tube first. Transfer as much heat as possible through the tube into the valve. Avoid prolonged heating of the valve itself.

5 Use just enough solder: with wire solder, use ¾" for a ¾" valve, etc. If too much solder is used, it may flow past the tube stop and clog the seating area.

6 Remove excess solder with a small brush while it is still plastic, leaving a fillet around the end of the valve as it cools.

Plastic pipe. Makers of plastic pipe object to the name plastic being applied to their product, because it has an undesirable connotation of poor quality, but it seems here to stay. Actually, though, the plastic used is far from being undesirable.

Plastic has probably made its greatest inroads in home plumbing systems in DWV applications. Like its counterpart in water pipe, DWV pipe is light, easy to cut with a hacksaw, and easy to join with a special primer and cement. It may be supported with the same kinds of hangers as metal pipe (band iron is my favorite), but care must be taken that the hangers don't cut into the pipe. As on other types of pipe, the hangers must be placed a certain distance apart depending on pipe diameter and if the material is installed horizontally; hangers must normally be used every 3' if the pipe is 3" in diameter and every 5' if the pipe is 5" in diameter.

If installing the material as sewer line to a cesspool or septic system, the pipe must be firmly supported in the trench it lies in with a select backfill.

Of the various types of plastic available, the most popular for waste and sewer uses are PVC (polyvinyl chloride) and ABS (acrylonitrile-butadiene-styrene). They come in lengths of 10' and 20' and in diameters of 1¼", 1½", 2", 3", and 4".

Fiber pipe. Another kind of pipe that is used in the drainage system is fiber pipe. This is made of cellulose wood fiber. It comes in a variety of diameters and lengths and is designed for use outside the house to carry water from gutters or sewage to the septic system or cesspool. The product that the Bermico

Working with plastic pipe: Cut it with a hacksaw; apply special primer, then adhesive; join firmly. A plastic joint cannot be taken apart.

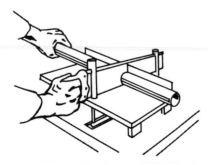

Company makes was once known as Orangeburg Pipe, a brand name; it is the same product.

This material is easy for the do-it-yourselfer to work with and Bermico provides instructions on its use.

It should be noted that some municipalities have codes that restrict the use of fiber pipe, particularly when sewage disposal is involved.

Water Pipe

Many of the same materials used for drainage systems are also used for water pipe, but they are, of course, available in smaller diameters. For the average home, pipe runs throughout the house are ½"; the main pipe coming into the house is usually ¾".

Galvanized pipe. Many older homes have a galvanized water pipe system, but it is not much used on new work anymore. Like any galvanized pipe, it must be threaded; it also has a tendency to scale and pit. On the other hand, it is strong—it resists water hammer and pressure well and rarely leaks. Galvanized should not be installed underground.

Common sizes of galvanized are, ⅜", ½", ¾", and 1". It is normally available in lengths of 21'; like galvanized drain pipe it must be cut to length and threaded.

When replacing a galvanized section of pipe, plumbers usually use copper tube instead. Fittings are available to join it with copper. If galvanized needs to be cut, a snap cutter works well.

Copper tubing. Copper pipe for the water supply is known as tubing. It comes in three classifications, K, L, and M, which refer to the wall thickness.

Type K, which comes in rigid lengths and flexible coils, is not used inside the house but rather is designed to be buried in the ground. Do-it-yourselfers rarely get involved with this.

Type L is what is used inside the house. It is available in rigid lengths and coils, but the rigid material also comes in type BT, or bending temper. The pipe can be bent with a special bending tool. This is expensive, however (around $50), so most do-it-yourselfers opt for straight runs with fittings.

Type M is used for heating applications and is not a factor in the home for water supply.

Rigid tubing comes in lengths of 10' and 20' and in diameters of from ¼" to 2", though more than 1" will not likely be needed. You can get coils cut to any length you wish.

Copper tubing can be joined with compression fittings, flare fittings, and by sweating or soldering. Sweating is the most popular method. As mentioned for waste pipe, the key is cleanliness and the pipe must be dry. A good trick to get water out of a pipe near the joint you are sweating is to soak it up with a piece of bread.

Plastic pipe. Plastic for water pipe may be polyethelene (PE)—a flexible material available in several densities—rigid PVC, polybutelene, or CPVC (chlorinated polyvinyl chloride). This latter pipe can be used for both hot and cold water systems, whereas the others cannot.

Plastic is available in all the same common sizes as other pipe and can be joined with other types with appropriate fittings (they're called transition fittings). It has the same advantages as drain pipe in terms of workability—it cuts easily, is lightweight, and glues together. Some plumbers do not use CPVC for hot water, saying it has a tendency to "spaghetti" (lose its rigidity). CPVC is rated for 180° F.

Plastic is commonly available in lengths of 10' and 20' and in various diameters. Let me emphasize, with the proper fittings plastic can be used to replace literally any kind of metal pipe in the house—water or drain—as long as local codes permit. A company that gears itself to the do-it-yourselfer is Genova.

Brass pipe. Brass for water is used where the water is especially corrosive. This is sturdy pipe and is usually joined by threaded couplings. Its big drawback is that it is prohibitively expensive.

If you work with it, use a strap wrench. This protects its shiny finish. Brass pipe may be connected with ordinary fittings except when joined to galvanized. Here special connectors called dielectric couplings must be used, or there will be harmful metallic interaction. This action—called electrolysis—takes a long time to occur (fifteen to twenty years), and some people don't use the dielectric couplings because they are so expensive.

Fittings

Fittings are used with drain and water pipe to do a number of different jobs: (*a*) to change the direction of the pipe, such as from a horizontal to a vertical run; (*b*) to accept another pipe; (*c*) to connect straight pieces of pipe; (*d*) to connect pieces of pipe made of different materials, such as connecting galvanized to copper, or cast-iron drain pipe to Transite—a cement-coated pipe used outside the house.

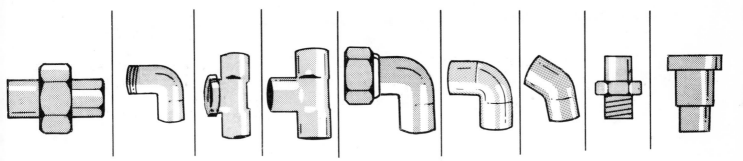

Typical copper fittings. From left to right: union, 90° male elbow, female tee, tee, 90° female elbow, 90° elbow, 45° elbow, male adapter and female adapter.

There is a wide variety of fittings available for use with all kinds of pipe, both water and waste, but the shapes tend to be the same; only the sizes and names differ. It is safe to say that you can get a fitting for whatever job is to be done.

Following is a roundup of common ones:

Nipples. These are short pipe sections. Around the home, these range in length from 1⅜″ up to about 1′. Nipples can be used wherever short sections of pipe are needed.

Couplings. These are for connecting pipes of the same or similar size that will be permanently connected.

Unions. These are for joining pipes that you expect to be disconnected.

Reducing couplings. These are for connecting pipes of different sizes that will not have to be disconnected. For example, you may be going from 2″ galvanized pipe to 1½″ copper going into the wall or floor, a common situation for under the kitchen sink.

Sweep. This is a curved piece of pipe mostly used as a waste fitting where you want the waste line to make a long, 90° turn.

Quarter bend. Also for waste where you want the pipe to make a 90° turn.

Wye. This looks like the letter Y and is mainly used to accept two pipes, one in each leg of the Y. It is a common waste fitting under a double sink where there are two drain lines.

Elbows (45° and 90°). Elbows join pipes at angles of either 45° or 90°.

Transition fittings—plastic to metal piping

Female Iron Pipe Adapter
for straight connections to male
iron pipe threads

Copper Tubing Adapter
for straight connections to copper
tubing, using a compression ring

Male Iron Pipe Adapter
for straight connections to female
iron pipe threads

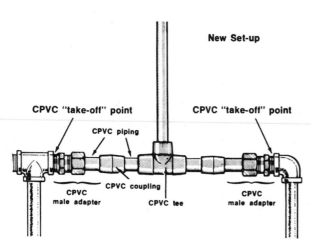

New Set-up

CPVC "take-off" point

CPVC piping

CPVC "take-off" point

CPVC
male adapter

CPVC coupling

CPVC tee

CPVC
male adapter

Here plastic hot water pipe is joined to
galvanized pipe with fittings designed for
the purpose.

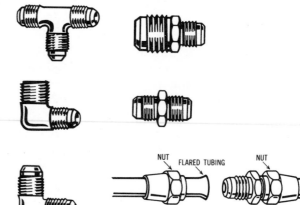

NUT   FLARED TUBING   NUT

Flare fittings

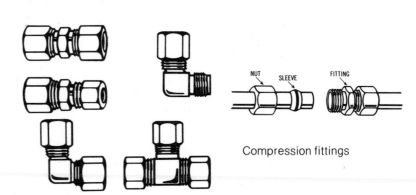

NUT   SLEEVE   FITTING

Compression fittings

166

Adapter. One end of this fitting is larger than the other, so it lets you join pipes of different sizes, and also different types of pipe. For example, a cast-iron-to-copper adapter is threaded onto the cast-iron end (or gasket) and is sweated at the copper end.

Street L and street 45. These are used where waste or water pipes emerge from the house.

Fittings are available in a variety of sizes for all types of pipe used around the house. They are commonly available in sizes of ½″ to 4″. As mentioned earlier, they are always female. The pipe goes inside the fitting (it's glued, screwed, or sweated) except in the case of no-hub cast-iron pipe, where clamps are used.

Valves

Valves in the house vary in style. On pipes there is usually one of three different kinds, a globe valve, a gate valve, or a ball valve. In essence, any valve functions like a faucet. A handle or lever is turned and a mechanism inside the valve restricts or stops water flow.

Of the three types, the gate valve and the globe valve are standard. A relative newcomer to the scene is the ball valve.

Gate Valve

This valve has a faucetlike handle attached to a metal wedge that seats in the bottom of the valve. When the handle is turned, the wedge is lifted, and the valve opens completely. There is an almost unrestricted flow of water.

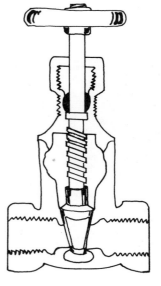

Inside a gate valve.

Gate valve

Globe Valve

This is even more like a faucet in construction. It has a stem on which there is a washer that is screwed down onto a seat. When lifted, the water flows.

Of the two types—gate and globe—the gate valve is better, simply because it allows almost unrestricted water flow.

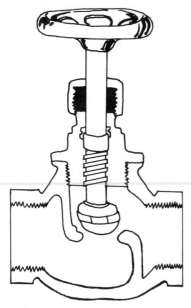

Inside a globe valve

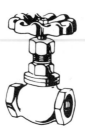

Globe valve.

Ball Valve

This is the best valve of all. It has a lever handle. When you turn it, a hollow ball inside the valve is turned and covers or uncovers a hole where the water flows from. It is the most positive shutoff of the three. Internal parts are Teflon coated, and it doesn't wear like the other two. It costs more (about 15 percent) than the gate valve, which in turn costs more than the globe valve.

Valves on pipe runs are made of either cast brass or plastic.

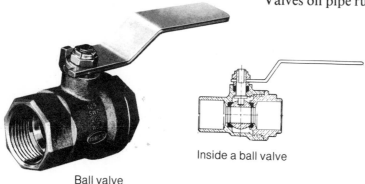

Ball valve

Inside a ball valve

Speedy Valves

Most sinks and toilets have valves to shut off the water flow. On a sink there are usually two valves, one for the hot water and one for the cold. Under the toilet there is a single valve.

Speedy valves (water supply valves)

Faucet valves commonly fasten to pipes coming out of the wall. The toilet valve may be linked with a pipe coming out of the wall or the floor.

In almost all cases the kind of valve used for faucets and toilets is the Speedy valve, so called because the water supply tubing it controls is called Speedy tubing. A Speedy valve is basically a globe valve. You turn the handle, and the end of a stem with a washer screws into a seat.

INSTALLATION TIPS

Although it is possible to replace parts on globe and gate valves, it is not easy and is not recommended. Reason: The stem, the basic component, varies greatly in size from company to company. It's likely you won't be able to get the match needed.

It is far better to replace the entire valve. Valves on galvanized pipe are very difficult to replace simply because you need to cut the valve off with a hacksaw, then thread the cut ends of the pipe and screw the new valve in place. Unless you are very experienced at doing this type of thing, better leave it to a plumber.

The only situation where it might be practical is if the particular pipe you're working on has a union fitting on it. The nuts securing this can be unscrewed and the entire piece of pipe taken down to be worked on.

Replacing a valve on a copper tube is not difficult. The valve can be cut off with a hacksaw or tubing cutter and a new valve either sweated (soldered) on in place or you can make a double-end compression valve, that is, one with compression fittings inserted in both ends of the valve. This would be more expensive, though easier to do for most people, than soldering the valve in place.

Plastic pipe valves may also be replaced. Again, the valve is hacksawed off and a valve of the appropriate size glued on. If it is cold water pipe, a PVC valve may be used; hot water would require a valve made of CPVC, but this may be a questionable choice in terms of its ability to stand the heat.

If you wish, you may also replace a metal globe, or gate or ball valve with a plastic one. Here you would need adapter fittings.

Valves under the sink and toilet may also be replaced. The valves may be screwed in place, glued on, sweated on, or attached with compression fittings. The sweated kind can be sweated off with a propane torch, a plastic valve can be cut off, and the compression can be unscrewed.

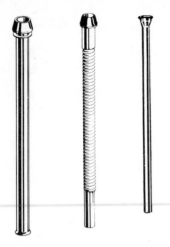

Various water supply tubes

Water Supply Tubes

When you replace a Speedy valve, you must ordinarily replace the water supply tube, unless you can make it fit with the new valve in place.

Water supply tubes for sinks may be flexible chrome-covered copper, rough brass (which is really uncoated copper), PVC plastic, or corrugated copper.

Of the four, the plastic is probably best for the do-it-yourselfer. It bends easily, and some bending will likely be required when connecting the water supply; rarely will it be the exact length required. Copper, either chrome plated or rough brass, can be all too easily kinked; and corrugated copper, which bends easily, only has a short section of straight run before it goes into the valve. In other words, the corrugated kind can be too short.

PVC can be cut with a hacksaw and attached with plastic adapters if you are attaching it to metal pipe. If you use copper, it is suggested that you get a mini-tubing cutter. This cuts the material easily: All you do is snug it up on the pipe and twirl it around; the blade cuts through.

INSTALLATION TIPS

There are a variety of ways that the water supply tubes are connected to the faucets and the valves. Common ones are shown in the illustrations.

Various ways water supplies are hooked up to threaded faucet shanks. Your best bet is to diassemble the supply and bring it into the store to get the necessary hardware.

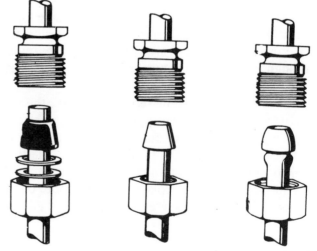

Toilet Parts

The flush toilet has not changed drastically since it was invented in the nineteenth century by Thomas Crapper in England. While the mechanical innards of the tank may look complicated when you look at them, the operation is a marvel of ingenious simplicity once you understand it. Essentially, the mechanism releases water (usually five gallons) into the tank to flush the bowl and to refill it.

How a Toilet Mechanism Works

Before you work on it, an understanding of its operation is required. An explanation follows. It is suggested that you read it through, then flush the toilet a few times and observe the operation of the tank parts.

The handle has a rod, called a trip lever, connected to it. Connected to the end of the lever are a couple of linked vertical rods or a chain. At the end of the rod or chain is the tank ball, which sits in a hole, called the flush valve seat, in the bottom of the tank. When you push the handle down, the trip lever lifts the rod or chain lifting the ball off the hole, water rushes out of the tank, flushing the bowl.

The tank is refilled by the action of the ball cock. As the water level in the tank lowers, a float ball goes down with it. This float ball is screwed to a rod that is linked on the end to the ball cock mechanism; specifically to a plungerlike part inside the ball cock. The plungerlike device lifts off a hole inside the ball cock as the water goes down, and water starts to rush out a tube that is part of the mechanism and into the tank when the plunger device is off it enough. At the same time the valve ball drops into the hole, the flush valve seats in the bottom of the tank, sealing it. As the water level in the tank rises, so does the tank ball, and the plunger is gradually pushed closed by the rod it is attached to. There is an overflow tube so that the tank can't fill to the point of overflowing. Also, a small refill tube from the ball cock simultaneously fills the bowl.

Every part inside a toilet tank is replaceable. Let's break them down and consider each.

Ball Cock

There are, conservatively speaking, over one-hundred makers of ball cock mechanisms. If a ball cock is faulty, you

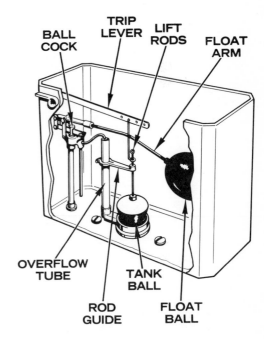

Toilet tank components

Ball cock isolated from other parts. It controls water flow.

can replace any one of the parts in the mechanism—washer, stem, and so forth—but this can be very difficult because there are many different makers and you may not be able to get the specific part (of course, in the interest of cost savings, you can try if you wish).

A far better idea is to replace the entire ball cock. Almost all the different makes will fit the same toilet. The main exception is the ball cock on a one-piece toilet; that is, one where tank and bowl are molded from one piece. This can be a very difficult job, and it is advised that a plumber be called in unless you are very handy.

INSTALLATION TIPS

If you buy a ball cock loose at the plumbing supply store, it will come with a float rod and refill tube. It is also available this way packaged, with instructions for installation, as well as with other necessary parts—float ball and tank ball, for example.

At any rate, replacing it is simple. You just use a wrench to loosen the locknut under the tank that secures the ball cock, and the large nut where the water supply connects to the threaded shank of the mechanism.

Once these two nuts are free, you can lift the mechanism out of the tank (you should turn off the water and flush the bowl before doing this) after disconnecting the bowl refill tube, which is screwed onto the ball cock.

To install the new ball cock, simply stick its shank through the hole in the tank and tighten the nuts.

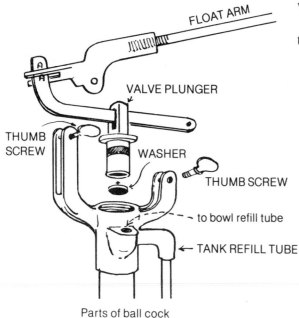

Parts of ball cock

Loosening nuts on water supply will release ball cock.

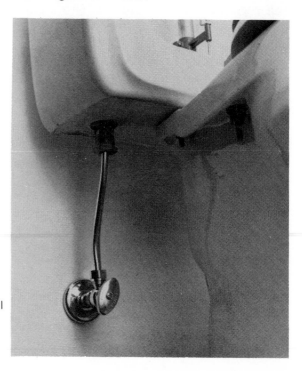

Fluidmaster

Over the last few years a new kind of ball cock mechanism called the Fluidmaster, which originated on the West Coast, has become very popular. This is essentially an all plastic unit that uses water pressure to control water flow into the tank.

This mechanism is preferred by many people. It is cheaper than a standard ball cock and quieter in operation. It is installed easily with plastic nuts and will fit in the vast majority of toilet tanks. It comes in two types. One has an antisiphon feature, which ensures that the tank water cannot back up through the ball cock into the water supply.

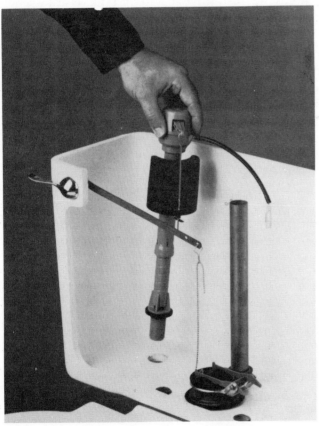

Fluidmaster unit slips into hole in tank where ball cock was mounted.

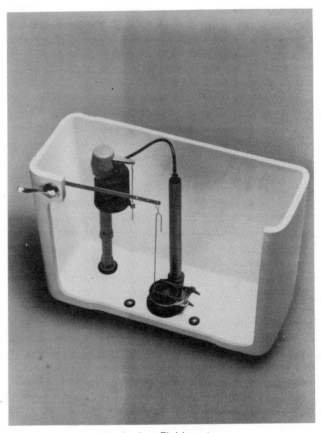

Hooked-up Fluidmaster

Flush Valve

A common toilet problem is that tank water leaks into the bowl because the valve seat gets corroded. There are two kinds of flush valve seats. One type is installed on toilets where the unit is connected to the tank, and the tank sits on a short elbow

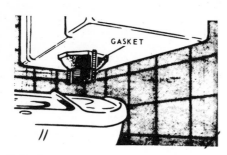

If flush valve is replaced, tank must be unbolted from toilet.

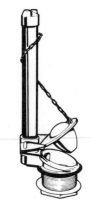

Flush valve with overflow tube

fitting. The other type is on the close-coupled toilet, meaning that the tank sits on the end of the bowl.

Replacing a flush valve seat in a toilet with a flush elbow is difficult and requires a special tool called a spud wrench to do the job. Unless you are very handy, it is definitely a job for a plumber.

For the other kind of toilet, where the tank sits on the bowl, the flush valve can be replaced fairly easily. As with any replacement, first turn off the water. Flush the toilet, then disconnect the seat from the bowl by loosening the two bolts that hold it on. Disconnect the water supply tube, then lift off the tank. But take care—china is very delicate.

A locknut holds the flush valve seat to the tank. Use a wrench to loosen it, then simply take the valve out, first unscrewing the overflow tube by hand.

Flush valve seats are pretty much standard size, but to ensure that you get the right size, bring the unit in with you. Reverse the procedure for installing the new seat. It comes with an overflow tube, which screws in place.

Fluidmaster also makes a flush valve seat renewal kit that can save you the job of taking the toilet apart. With this you just secure a new stainless steel cup over the seat with epoxy tape. Detailed instructions come with the unit.

Flush valve renewal kit. Stainless steel ring is epoxy-taped to hole in bottom of tank. Black adapter ring is used if the seat is ceramic.

Flush Valve Ball

There are two kinds: the flapper type, which is attached to the overflow tube, and the type that is just attached to the chain or lift rod. They come in various shapes.

The flapper ball is the best kind to get. One size, 2½″, will fit all toilets. Some of these are attached to the overflow tube, while some attach to the flush valve seat. They are not difficult to install. Installation instructions come on the package. A chain is included. If chain or guide rods are needed, these are available separately or in sets.

Refill Tube

This comes in one standard size. If it goes, just get another like it and screw it to the ball cock.

Overflow Tube

Made from tubular copper that is chrome plated, this usually rots out before the flush valve seat. It usually comes with the flush valve; if not, it is available singly. The end that screws in is normally either 1″ or 1⅛″ in diameter. It's a simple matter, however, to bring the overflow with you when you go to the store. These come in a couple of gauges. Get the heaviest.

A variety of flush valve balls are available, but the best is the flapper ball *(bottom)*.

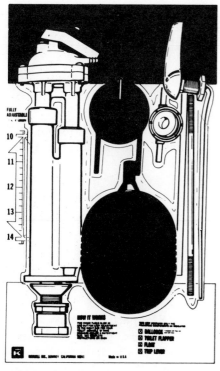

Kits are also available for repairing toilet tanks.

If the toilet needs to be plunged, a plunger with a retractable bulb on the end is good. The bulb is retracted when using the device on the sink.

Toilet hinges are also available, but it's usually more economical simply to buy a new seat.

Handle

The handle actually consists of the part that projects from the toilet and a horizontal rod—trip lever—that is connected to either the lift rod or the chain. When removing the existing handle, turn it *clockwise*. Unlike most items, handles are threaded counterclockwise and tighten with a counterclockwise motion. Otherwise, the more the handle is used, the more it could loosen.

Float Ball

A common problem is that the ball gets water logged. Float balls are almost always the same size no matter who makes them. Standard size is 2½" in diameter; a few are 3". There may be copper ones available, but they are difficult to get. Today almost all are plastic.

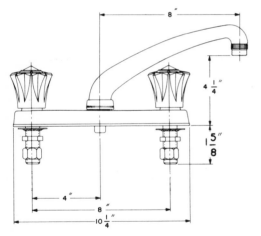

Sinks are usually on 8" centers.

Sink and Lavatory Faucets

Faucets are available in a tremendous array of styles and colors. Indeed, you can even get ones that are shaped like fish and other creatures and are gold plated.

The main sinks you'll be concerned with are the kitchen sink and the lavatory, or bathroom basin. No matter the style, installation is essentially the same.

Kitchen sinks may be wall mounted or deck mounted. That is, the water supply pipes may sprout from the wall, or the faucet may sit on the deck, with water connections under the sink.

The key dimension in replacing a faucet is knowing what center-to-center measurements, or "centers," are. This is the distance between the center of the hot water handle and the center of the cold water one.

Kitchen sink faucets are usually 8" apart but may be 6". Lavatory faucets are usually on 4" centers, but 8" is not uncommon. If you are replacing a faucet, and have any doubt about the size, by all means bring the faucet into the store with you. Wall-mounted lavatory faucets are usually 4½" but may be 6".

Faucets are usually made of chrome-plated brass, but there are also chrome-plated plastic models and plain plastic ones. The latter, referred to in the trade as "builder's specials," are inferior products. Chrome-plated plastic is good. Delex is one brand.

Chrome-plated brass comes in two materials: tubular and cast brass. The cast variety is much better.

Chrome-plated pot metal is also available, but it is inferior and rots out quite readily. Because of the chrome coating it is difficult to tell, at least from surface appearance, whether or not a faucet is made of pot metal. However, if you heft a cast brass faucet and a pot metal one, there will be a noticeable difference in weight; the cast brass one will be much heavier.

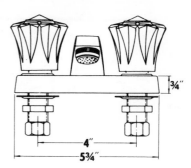

Lavatory faucets (basins) are usually on 4" centers.

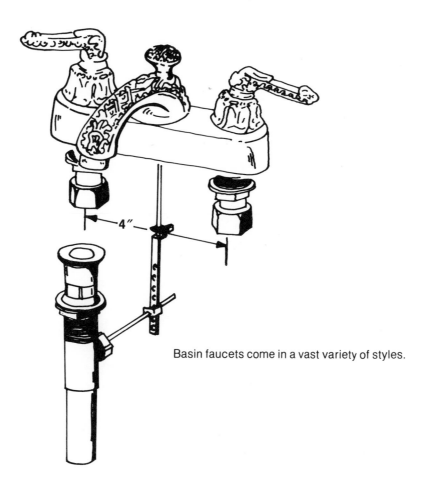

Basin faucets come in a vast variety of styles.

INSTALLATION TIPS

Compression faucets may be replaced relatively easily. All that needs to be done, basically, is to loosen the locknuts that secure the faucet to the deck, then loosen the nuts that connect the faucet shank to the water supply tubes: Do the latter first. A basin wrench is usually needed because the nuts are jammed up

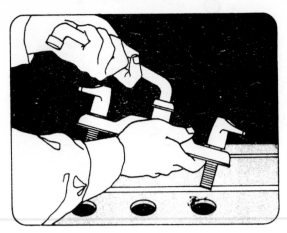

Faucet shanks are slipped through holes
in the sink to install.

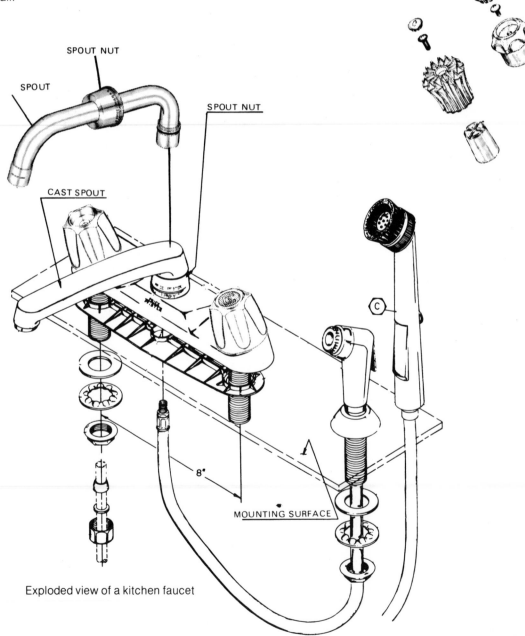

SPOUT NUT

SPOUT

SPOUT NUT

CAST SPOUT

8"

MOUNTING SURFACE

C

Exploded view of a kitchen faucet

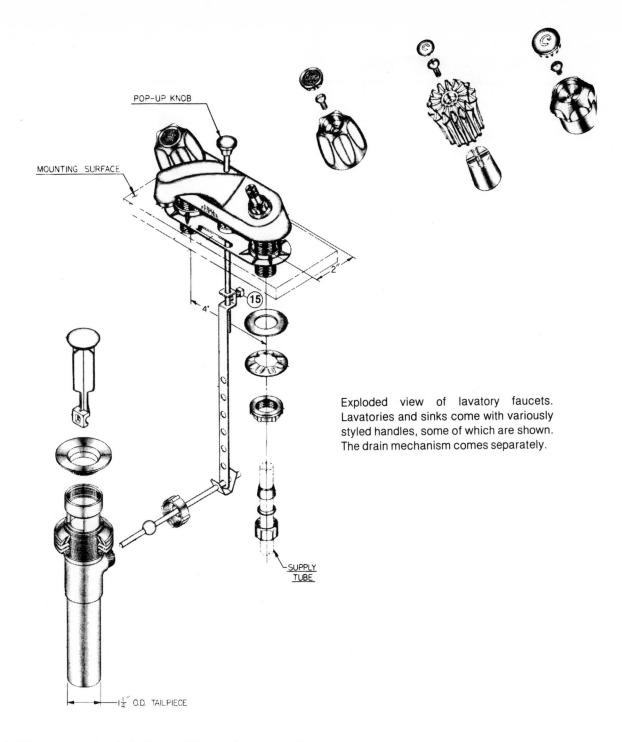

POP-UP KNOB

MOUNTING SURFACE

2"

4"

(15)

SUPPLY
TUBE

1¼" O.D. TAILPIECE

Exploded view of lavatory faucets.
Lavatories and sinks come with variously
styled handles, some of which are shown.
The drain mechanism comes separately.

behind the back of the bowl. The basin wrench has a serrated
hooklike handle that enables it to get a tight grip on the nuts for
turning.

When the faucet is loose, it is lifted out and the supply tubes
are moved out of the way, or discarded if they're not long
enough. To install the new faucet, its threaded shanks are
passed through the holes in the deck. Each water supply tube
usually has a compression fitting. It has a bulbed end and
ferrule that slips inside each shank. It is jammed up against the

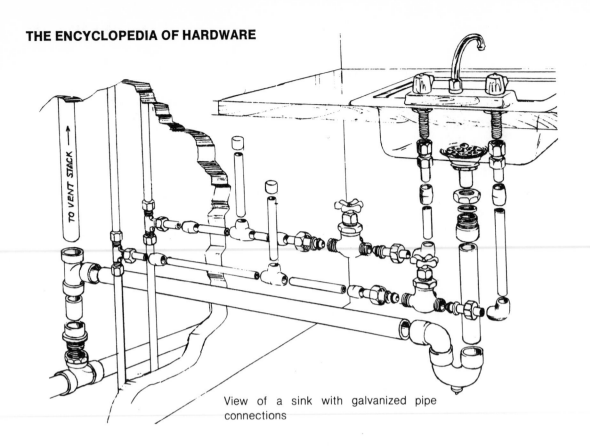

View of a sink with galvanized pipe connections

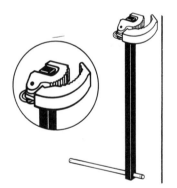

A basin wrench is handy for removing nuts that secure the faucet to the sink.

shank. When the fitting nut is tightened, the connection is made watertight. Other ways of connecting the water supply are shown in the sketches.

You may replace the faucets with any kind that has the correct center-to-center measurements. In most cases putty must be applied under the base of the faucet; in other cases a rubber gasket is used. You could also use the method for installing faucets in a new sink or basin. Again, it just depends on the center-to-center measurements. Faucets commonly come with installation instructions.

Faucet Repair

A compression faucet works simply. Inside the faucet body there is a threaded stem on the end of which is a washer held on by a brass screw. This washer sits in a hole where the water comes from. A handle controls the stem action. Turning the handle to *Off* makes the washer press down against the hole—called a seat—sealing off water. Turning the handle to *On* lifts the stem off the seat, and water flows.

All the parts on faucets are usually replaceable. Taking a faucet apart to get at them is not difficult. First you turn off the water. Disassembly may vary a bit. On many you just loosen a chrome packing nut on the faucet (put tape over it to protect it), then turn the handle in the *On* direction until the stem comes up and out. On other types you have to remove the handle first (it's attached by a screw on top) in order to expose the stem, which has a nut built onto it. Turning this will release the stem. On still other types you remove the handle, then reinsert it and turn the stem out. There is really no mystery to it. You turn things that look like they can be turned, and the faucet comes apart.

Now, let's consider compression faucet replacement parts.

Stems

The number of different faucet stems is in the hundreds, perhaps thousands. Wrightway Manufacturing, for example, devotes almost all of a thick catalogue to various sizes.

The best bet, then, is to bring the stem into the plumbing supply store for a match. Or if you have the schematic drawing that comes with the faucet, bring this. It is not enough just to tell the dealer that you have, say, an American Standard Brand kitchen faucet. Even within one manufacturer there is great variation.

Handles

Here again manufacturers make many different kinds, so handles can be hard to replace, unless they are a popular style. Bring the handle into the store to get either a duplicate or one that fits the faucet. If you can't get either one of these, many manufacturers, such as Melard and Plumbcraft, make handles that will fit over the top of any stem. The handle is slipped over the stem and then a small Allen wrench (provided) is used to tighten a screw or screws to secure it. Usually when the handle slips, the stem is also ruined and must be replaced.

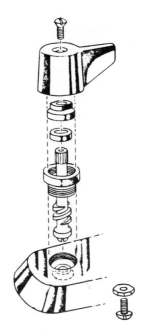

Cut away of compression faucet. Worm-gear-like stem has washer on bottom that covers—or uncovers—seat hole where water flows from.

Faucet stem

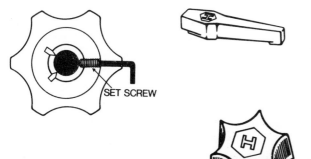

SET SCREW

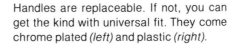

Handles are replaceable. If not, you can get the kind with universal fit. They come chrome plated *(left)* and plastic *(right)*.

Beveled and flat washers. Install flat washers with embossed printing up.

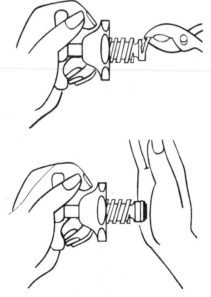

No-rotate washer

Method of replacing a no-rotate washer. The rim on the stem is pulled or filed off, then the washer is snapped in place.

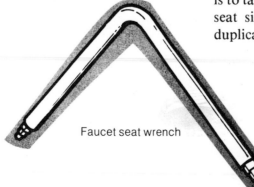

Faucet seat wrench

Washers

There are two standard kinds of washers for faucets: flat and beveled. They are usually made of neoprene, a kind of plastic, but may also be rubber. Neoprene is better.

New faucets commonly come with flat washers, simply because these make better contact with the seat than the beveled kind. On a repair job, however, the beveled kind is preferred. The seat that the washer pushes against is usually pitted, and the beveled kind seals better.

Washers come in a variety of sizes. Plumbers commonly buy assorted sizes in boxes of one-hundred. However, a large assortment of washers is usually a bad investment for the do-it-yourselfer, simply because the average house will never require them all. Far better is a small assortment. These are commonly available twelve and twenty to the box. There are usually two or three sizes, with a few brass screws included, and you're likely to get one that will fit. Manufacturers commonly make washers in different sizes, even though they may have the same nominal size. For example, a so-called "quarter" washer in one brand will be a different size in another. The only way to ensure that a washer will fit is to try it.

In some cases the cup, or rim, on the stem where the washer is mounted will be so worn that an ordinary washer will not seal, and you will have difficulty getting the right size stem. Here it is suggested that you get a no-rotate washer. It consists of a cup with a washer. First, you file or pull off the stem (with pliers) then snap the washer into the screwhole in the stem. It doesn't rotate like a regular washer and therefore doesn't get the same kind of wear.

Seats

Seats rival stems in the number of sizes available; there are hundreds. Manufacturers sell these in small assortments, a few to the package, but buying this way isn't really a good idea because only one of them will likely fit the faucet. Your best bet is to take the seat into a dealer. He has a metal board with many seat sizes threaded into it that should enable him to get a duplicate for you.

Replacing a seat is simple. It screws into the top of the water outlet. The inside of the seat has flat sides like a nut. An Allen wrench of an appropriate size is slipped in and turned; the seat sticks to it by friction, and you lift it up and out (a flashlight will enable you to see things better).

A better tool, though, is a faucet seat wrench. This is an L-shaped piece of metal that is tapered, with flat sides. It can fit any size seat.

To install the new seat, reverse the procedure. Slip the new seat on the wrench and simply screw it back into place.

You must be gentle with either of the above tools so as not to deform the seat (they're made of brass and may be old). An even better tool for removal is the screw extractor, which bites into the seat to unscrew it; the danger of deforming it is minimal. Use a faucet or Allen wrench to replace the seat.

Aerators and strainers are also replaceable on sinks. Aerators can be hard to fit: If you can't get the exact size, bring the aerator to the dealer. There are ones available, such as from Melard, which are a universal fitting type. Strainers are usually a standard size, but these also should be brought to the dealer to get the correct one. Some types require that a locknut that holds the strainer to the sink be turned while a helper holds the handles on a plier in the cross-hatching of the strainer so the unit doesn't turn.

Some faucets do not come with replaceable seats. When the seat gets worn, therefore, there's nothing to do except replace the entire faucet. It's important, then, when buying a faucet, to get the renewable kind.

Faucet seats come in a tremendous array of sizes. Shown are just four.

Aerators come in various sizes. Your best bet is to bring the old unit in for a replacement.

Aerator from Melard will fit any faucet spout.

A strainer on a sink can be installed by screwing it into place.

Spouts

On a kitchen faucet the spout is usually replaceable. Almost all of them can be screwed off by hand. To do this you'll have to remove the faucet handles so they won't obstruct the turn.

Washerless Faucets

In addition to the compression faucet, there are so-called washerless faucets. (Actually, there is no faucet without a seat or washerlike device that isn't replaceable.) These may be either a cartridge or a ball type. Typically, there is a ball with holes in it inside the faucet body. When the faucet is open, the holes on the ball are lined up with those in the faucet body so that water can flow. When closed, the holes are not lined up.

Such faucets can also be fixed, but they vary so much from one maker to the next that you should get repair parts based on specific makes, such as Peerless or Aqualine. Such companies have kits, complete with instructions and parts available. If one part goes bad, it is likely that other parts will soon follow, so it would be best to replace all the internal parts at the same time.

Various replacement parts for drainage on the sink or lavatory. As with most plumbing parts, bring the old part in to the dealer to get the correct replacement.

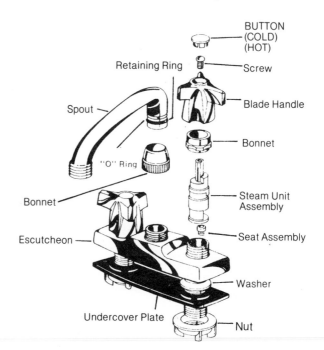

Exploded view of a washerless faucet

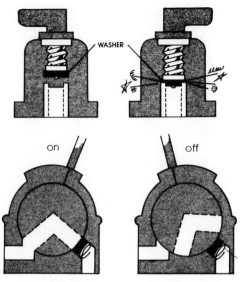

Repair kit for a washerless faucet. You must get the parts or a kit from the manufacturer of your specific faucet.

These are the ways a compression faucet *(above)* and washerless faucet *(below)* work. In the compression type the faucet presses down on the seat. In the washerless type a ball slides across a hole to plug it up.

Single-Handle Faucets

Single-handle faucets are also sold. By manipulating the handle you can control either hot or cold water or mix the two. Such faucets are always washerless.

Washerless, single-handle, and double-handle faucets are also available for baths and kitchens (and other sinks) in kits complete with installation instructions. There is no question that they will last longer than compression types, so this might be something you'll want to consider.

Traps and Other Sink Parts

Traps are designed to trap water, providing a seal against gas and vermin getting into the house through drain holes. Most common for sinks and basins are P-traps and S-traps, so called because they are shaped like those particular letters. A P-trap is used between the sink and the wall; an S-trap is used between the sink and the floor.

Traps are prime spots to look at when a sink is clogged. Removing them and cleaning them out, or using a snake to probe further down the drain line, usually solves the problem.

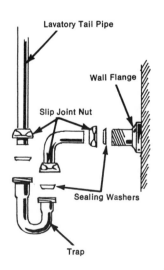

Exploded view of a P-trap and connections

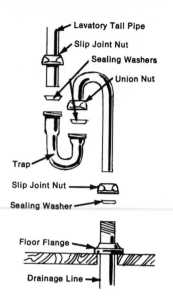

Exploded view of an S-trap and connections

Traps may be made of copper, brass, or galvanized iron. A recent development that shows promise is a clear plastic trap. This enables one to see a blockage instantly.

Traps are secured by slipnuts. To remove the trap, you unscrew the nuts by hand or with a wrench, then slip them up out of the way. Get a replacement trap the same size and reverse the procedure to install it.

Some S-traps come with a cleanout plug. You just unscrew this to clean the trap out. Actually, a plug is a bad idea because when a trap gets old, this plug, which is screwed in, can be difficult to turn. In doing so, the pipes around it can be bent.

Traps are standard sizes. The kitchen sink trap normally has a diameter of $1\frac{1}{2}'' \times 1\frac{1}{2}''$; the basin is $1\frac{1}{2}'' \times 1\frac{1}{4}''$, or, rarely, $1\frac{1}{4}'' \times 1\frac{1}{4}''$.

Other Sink Parts

In addition to the trap, there are a number of other pieces on a sink that can be replaced.

One such is the strainer, which screws into the drain hole in the sink. This is normally $3\frac{1}{2}''$ in diameter and can be removed and replaced either by loosening the large nut on the underside of the sink that holds it on or by sticking a pair of screwdriver blades under the strainer, then using another screwdriver or bar to turn it out.

Strainers are sold singly and are installed by screwing them back in place and retightening the nut. First, though, a bead of plumber's putty should be laid under the lip of the strainer for watertightness.

Running down from the strainer is the tailpiece, which is connected to the strainer by another nut. The tailpiece is usually connected to another short section of pipe called a J-bend. This links up directly with another piece of pipe going into the wall if a "P" trap or a "S" trap is going into the floor.

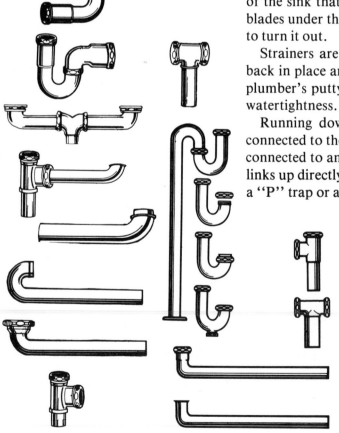

Pipe and tubing for undersink connections come in a variety of sizes and configurations. They can be unscrewed by hand or wrench and brought in for replacement.

Those just discussed are the standard connections. On other sinks and basins there may be other pipes of various configurations. But these sections, too, may be replaced. You can use the original material—say, brass—but plastic may also be used. However, where a pipe under the sink is exposed, such as on a basin, it is likely that you will have chrome-plated brass and may want to stick with this for good looks.

On the lavatory there is another part that can be replaced—the P.O. assembly, or pop-up drain mechanism. To remove and replace this:

1. Remove the trap. This will give you room to work.

2. Remove the rod that is attached to the pop-up drain. This will be secured by a clip or setscrew.

3. Use a wrench to loosen the locknut that secures the assembly to the basin; unscrew the pop-up.

This part comes in brass or pot metal. Brass of course, is much better.

Tub Parts

The parts one can repair or replace on a tub are the faucets and related parts and the drain mechanism. Following is a consideration of each.

Tub and shower faucets usually come several different ways: three-valve diverters, two-valve diverters, two-valve shower fittings or two-valve tub fillers, and single-control tub and shower units.

A three-valve diverter has hot and cold water faucets, termed valves, and a faucet (valve) in the middle for diverting the water from the shower to the bath. The two-valve diverter has hot and cold water faucets and a pop-up device on the spout for diverting the water as needed. The two-valve shower fitting has hot and cold water faucets for a shower only. The two-valve tub filler has hot and cold water faucets for filling the tub. The single-control has, as its name implies, one handle.

Standard tub-faucet center-to-center measurements are 8". Six inches or 11" may also be used. This is when they are wall mounted. On the old freestanding tub, where the plumbing is exposed, the measurement is usually 3½".

If you are replacing a tub faucet, it will be a big job if you have to open up a tile wall. In many cases you can avoid this, however, by checking a closet or open area behind the faucet. Many times there will be a panel with access to the tub fittings. Even if there isn't, it will be less of job to cut through a wall material such as Sheetrock than to go through the tile.

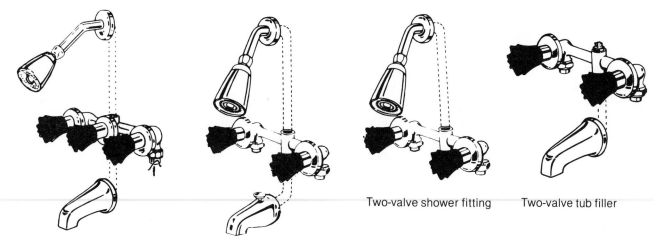

Three-valve (faucet) diverter faucet   Two-valve diverter   Two-valve shower fitting   Two-valve tub filler

Instructions for assembling the faucet will be on the package, but how to attach it to the existing piping will depend on what is there. Faucets can be attached to iron (threaded) pipe or to copper, and you buy the unit with fittings that will be sweated or screwed on. Faucets are commonly available for attaching to ½″ pipe.

Faucets are available in chrome-plated brass, chrome-plated plastic, chrome-plated pot metal, and plain plastic. Brass is best; pot metal and plain plastic are inferior.

Faucets are commonly the compression type. That is, there is a stem with a washer on it that presses against a seat, either renewable or not.

It is more difficult to remove the stem on a tub than on a sink. The handle must first be removed, then the decorative escutcheon plate unscrewed. A packing nut is then usually removed and a socket wrench used to turn a bonnet nut that is built onto the stem.

Sets of socket wrenches—about ten sockets in all because sizes differ—can be rented from plumbing supply houses. Or you can measure the bonnet nut and buy a specific size to fit.

Like sink faucet stems, tub stems are made in a vast array of sizes, so your best bet is to bring the stem into the store to get a replacement.

O-rings *(top)* and stranded packing *(bottom)*

O-Rings

Some tub faucets also use O-rings. An O-ring is basically a round washer that is friction-fit around the stem and takes the

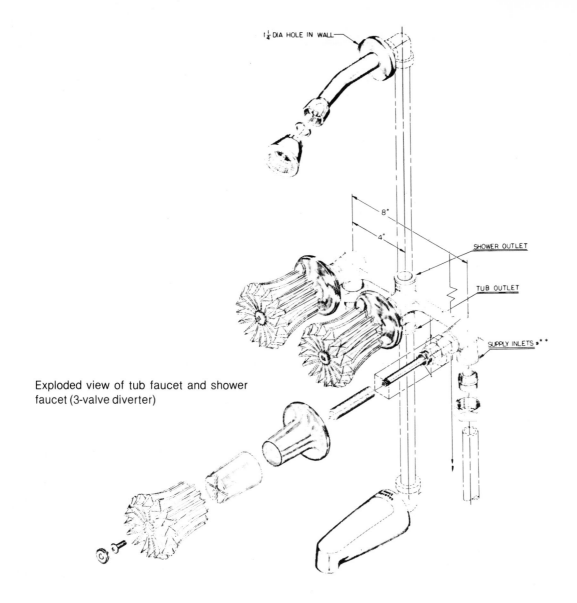

1¼ DIA HOLE IN WALL

8"

4"

SHOWER OUTLET

TUB OUTLET

SUPPLY INLETS

Exploded view of tub faucet and shower
faucet (3-valve diverter)

place of the packing. You can buy single O-rings or a small
assortment.

Tub faucets also may have packing. This can be replaced
simply.

Seats

Some seats on tub faucets are replaceable. You remove them
the same way as you do a sink faucet. Insert an Allen wrench or
seat wrench and turn it out. Or, better yet, use the screw extractor mentioned on page 80.

Handles

The handles on faucets are replaceable. Either you can get ones to match what you have or you can get the universal-fitting types, as on sinks.

Shower Heads

Shower heads are also replaceable. There are two kinds. The old type has a ball on the end of the shower arm; the head is attached to the ball. Here the arm and head are one piece. You can unscrew it; to avoid snapping it, hold the arm near the wall as you turn it near the front.

The new type of shower head is threaded on both ends. To replace the head, you merely have to unscrew it. Any shower head will fit it.

Shower arms can be unscrewed and replaced.

The new type of shower heads may be unscrewed. With the old type, the entire arm must come off.

Drain Mechanisms

There are two kinds of drain mechanisms commonly used in a tub: weight (piston) and spring. This latter type is used where there is no tub stopper.

The weight mechanism consists of an escutcheon through which a lever sticks. On the end of the lever, inside the drain pipe, is a linkage, at the bottom of which is a metal weight. Flip (or turn) the handle up and the weight lowers into a seat, blocking water flow. Push the handle down and the weight lifts off, allowing water flow.

This mechanism develops a variety of problems. In some cases, the lever doesn't stay down, in which case it is likely that a small spring that should keep the lever up is worn. The escutcheon and lever require replacement.

To remove the assembly, just unscrew it from the tub, then grasp the lever and lift the whole thing—lever handle and linkage with weight attached—up and out of the hole. Remove

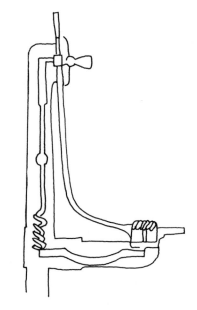

Spring-type mechanism

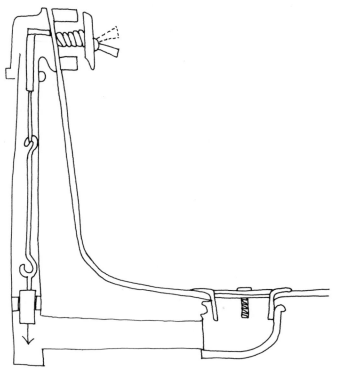

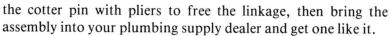

Weight-type drain mechanism

the cotter pin with pliers to free the linkage, then bring the assembly into your plumbing supply dealer and get one like it.

If a blockage develops with this type of mechanism, you can plunge the toilet (first block the overflow with sopping wet rag) or close the tub and pour some baking soda and hot water down into the drain, letting it sit for a while. Often grime collects on the seat and prevents snug sealing; the baking soda and water solution can break this up.

The spring-type mechanism is easy to spot. It has a chrome pop-up stopper. The spring mechanism also has a linkage, but on the end of it is a spring that presses against a rocker-arm assembly on the end of which is the pop-up drain. When you flip the lever, the spring pushes against the rocker arm and pushes up or closes the stopper.

A problem with this type of mechanism is that hair and debris collect on the spring. You can remove this the same way you would from the weight type, then clean off the spring and replace. If a lack of tension on the lever is the problem, the lever can be removed and replaced, as in the weight type.

If necessary, the drain on any tub may be removed and replaced. On some you can insert a screwdriver into the crosshatching of the drain and unscrew it; on other types a spud wrench is required to grip small projections on the inside of the drain for turning.

APPENDIX

I am grateful to the companies and organizations below for supplying information and/or illustrations for this book. I am also grateful to my son, Tom, who contributed quite a few drawings.

Acorn Manufacturing Company, Inc.
Mansfield, Massachusetts 12048

Adams Rite Manufacturing Company
4040 South Capitol Avenue
P. O. Box 1301
City of Industry, California 91749

Advanced Affiliates, Inc.
96–12 43rd Avenue
Corona, New York 11368

Afco Industires, Inc.
2801 South Post Oak Road
Suite 370
Houston, Texas 77027

Allen Manufacturing Company
P. O. Drawer 570
Hartford, Connecticut 06101

Allen - Stevens Conduit
   Fittings Corp.
29 Park Avenue
Manhasset, New York 11030

David Allison Company, Inc.
220 Crossways Park West
Woodbury, New York 11797

American Chain & Cable Company, Inc.
454 East Princess Street
York, Pennsylvania 17403

American Lock Company
Exchange Road & Kedzie Avenue
Crete, Illinois 60417

American Mason Safety Tread Company
88 Wellman Street
Lowell, Massachusetts 10851

American Screw
Wytheville, Virginia 24382

American Tack & Hardware Company, Inc.
25 Robert Pitt Drive
Monsey, New York 10952

Amerock Corp.
4000 Auburn
Rockford, Illinois 61101

Amoco Chemicals Corp.
1530 Commerce Drive
Stow, Ohio 44224

AMP Special Industries
Valley Forge, Pennsylvania 19482

Anchor Wire Corp.
   of Tennessee
425 Church Street
Goodlettsville, Tennessee 37072

Anderson Copper and Brass
3800 West 127th Street
Alsip, Illinois 60658

Apex Wire & Cable Corp.
380 Vanderbilt Motor Pkwy.
Hauppauge, New York 11787

Arrow Lock Corp.
4900 Glenwood Rd.
Brooklyn, New York. 11234

Arrowsmith Tool & Mfg. Company
9700 Bellanca Avenue
Los Angeles, California 90045

Artistic Brass
Division of Norris Industries
3136 East 11th St.
Los Angeles, California 90023

Atlantic Steel Company
Box 1714
Atlanta, Georgia 30301

The B & T Metals Company
Columbus, Ohio 43216

The Baden Steelbar and
   Bolt Corp. R-3
Sewickley, Pennsylvania 15143

Baldwin Hardware Mfg. Corp.
841 Wyomissing Blvd.
Reading, Pennsylvania 19603

Barclay Industries, Inc.
65 Industrial Road
Lodi, New Jersey 17644

Bassick Division
Stewart Warner Corp.
960 Atlantic
Bridgeport, Conn. 06602

Baron Manufacturing Company
2035 West Charleston St.
Chicago, Illinois 60647

Bead Chain Company
Mountain Grove & State Streets
Bridgeport, Connecticut 06605

Beeco Products, Inc.
P. O. Box 5366
Detroit, Michigan 48235

Belwith International, Ltd.
7600 Industry Avenue
Pico Rivera, California 90660

Bermico Company
P. O. Box 658
West Bend, Wisconsin 53095

The Bristol Brass Corp.
P. O. Box 1320
Bristol, Connecticut 06010

Brush Nail Expansion Bolt Company
P. O. Box 1338
Greenwich, Connecticut 16830

Bryant
Division of Westinghouse, Inc.
Bridgeport, Connecticut 06602

Bethlehem Steel Corp.
Bethlehem, Pennsylvania 18016

Blaine Window Hardware, Inc.
1919 Blaine Drive
RD 4
Hagerstown, Maryland 21740

The William L. Bonnell Company, Inc.
25 Bonnell Street
Newnan, Georgia 30263

Brewer Titchener Corp.
P. O. Box 832
Cortland, New York 13045

Builders Brass Works Corp.
3474 Union Pacific Ave.
Los Angeles, California 90023

CM Chain
Division Columbus McKinnon Corp.
Tonawanda, New York 14150

Cadillac Plastic & Chem Company
P. O. Box 810
Detroit, Michigan 48232

Camcar Division of Textron, Inc.
345 East Marshall Street
Wytheville, Virginia 24382

Cardinal Foundry & Supply Company
5200 Harvard Avenue
Cleveland, Ohio 44105

Cerro Copper Products
P. O. Box 681
East St. Louis, Illinois 62202

Cipco Corp.
Cole Street at 22nd
St. Louis, Missouri 63106

Clamp Nail Company
9333 Schiller Blvd.
Franklin Park, Illinois 60131

Cleveland Rubber & Plastic Company
5100 Terminal Street
P. O. Box 8730
Charlotte, North Carolina 28208

Corbin Cabinet Lock
Division of Emhart Corp.
Berlin, Connecticut 06037

Covert Manufacturing Company
P.O. Box 778
Troy, New York 12181

Crane Company
300 Park Avenue
New York, New York 10022

PCI Group, Inc.
Division of W. W. Cross
Industrial Park
Box B-976
New Bedford, Massachusetts 02741

Dalton Manufacturing Company
130 South Bemiston
St. Louis, Missouri 63105

W. J. Dennis & Company
1111 Davis Road
Elgin, Illinois 60120

Edward A. Designs, Inc.
42–81 Hunter Street
Long Island City, New York 11101

Dexter Lock
Division of Kysor Industrial Corp.
1601 Madison Ave. South East
Grand Rapids, Michigan 49507

Dick Brothers, Inc.
3rd & Buttonwood Streets
Reading, Pennsylvania 19603

Eagle Electric
45–31 Court Square
Long Island City, New York 11101

Eastern Chain Works, Inc.
144–150 West 18th Street
New York, New York 10011

R. E. Edwards & Associates
P. O. Box 3023
Oakland, California 94609

Elco Industries, Inc.
Consumer Products Division
1111 Samuelson Rd.
Rockford, Illinois 61101

Electracraft Manufacturing
  Company
24455 Aurora Road
Bedford Heights, Ohio 44146

Eljer Plumbingware
Wallace Murray Corp.
3 Gateway Center
Pittsburgh, Pennsylvania 15222

The Engineered Products Company
P. O. Box 108
Flint, Michigan 48501

EZ Plumb
P. O. Box 37
Plano, Texas 75074

Ferum
815 East 136th Street
Bronx, New York 10454

The Fox Police Lock Company
46 West 21st Street
New York, New York 10010

Gantt Manufacturing Company
230 Seventh Street
Macon, Georgia 31202

Gem Electric Manufacturing
  Company, Inc.
380 Vanderbilt Motor Parkway
Hauppauge, New York 11787

General Electric Company
Wiring Device Department
Providence, Rhode Island 02940

Genova, Inc.
7034 East Court Street
Davison, Michigan 48423

Gould Electrical, Inc.
Components Division
123 Smith Street
East Farmingdale, New York 11735

Grant Hardware Company
High Street
New York 10994

Gries Reproducer Company
125 Beechwood Ave.
New Rochelle, New York 10802

Groov-Pin Corp.
1125 Hendricks Causeway
Ridgefield, New Jersey 07657

Hager Hinge Company
139 Victor Street
St. Louis, Missouri 63104

Hand Tools Institute
331 Madison Avenue
New York, New York 10017

Handi-Man Fasteners
191 Fabyan Place
Newark, New Jersey 07112

Hardware Designers, Inc.
Mount Kisco, New York 10549

Harloc Products Corp.
West Haven, Connecticut 06516

Hart Products Company
P. O. Box 9
New Albany, Indiana 47150

The Hillwood Manufacturing Company
21700 St. Clair Ave.
Cleveland, Ohio 44117

Hindley Manufacturing Company, Inc.
Cumberland, Rhode Island 02864

Hy-Ko Products Company
24001 Aurora Road
Bedford Heights, Ohio 44146

Ideal Industries, Inc.
Sycamore, Illinois 60178

Independent Nail, Inc.
106 Hale Street
Bridgewater, Massachusetts 02324

Inryco, Inc.
Division of Milicor
4601 North Point Blvd.
Baltimore, Maryland 21219

I-T-E Imperial Corp.
Route 309
Norristown Road
Spring House, Pennsylvania 19477

Ideal Security Hardware Corp.
215 East Ninth Street
St. Paul, Minnesota 55101

Jaybee Manufacturing Corp.
2031 Huron Street
P. O. Box 54110
Los Angeles, California 90054

Jedco, Inc.
P. O. Box 604
Elkhart, Indiana 46514

Jefferson Screw Corp.
691 Broadway
New York, New York 10012

Jordan Industries, Inc.
3030 North West 75th Street
Miami, Florida 33147

Kason Hardware Corp.
Binghamton, New York 13902

Kindergard
3357 Halifax Street
Dallas, Texas 75247

Kinkead Industries, Inc.
5860 North Pulaski Road
Chicago, Illinois 60646

Kirsch Company
Sturgis, Michigan 49091

Klauer Manufacturing Company
P. O. Box 59
Dubuque, Iowa 52001

Knape and Vogt Manufacturing Company
2700 Oak Industrial Drive North East
Grand Rapids, Michigan 49505

Kohler Company
Kohler, Wisconsin 53044

La Belle Industies
500 South Worthington Street
Oconomowoc, Wisconsin 53066

Chas. O. Larsen Company
Sterling, Illinois 61081

Edward Leeds Company
Freeport, New York 11520

Lehigh Sales and Products, Inc.
1929 Vultee Street
Allentown, Pennsylvania 18105

Lenape Products, Inc.
Route 31
Pennington, New Jersey 08534

Leviton Manufacturing Company, Inc.
59–25 Little Neck Parkway
Little Neck, New York 11362

Loxem Manufacturing Corp.
1201 Exchange Drive
Richardson, Texas 75080

Lutron
Coopersburg, Pennsylvania 18036

Mapsco Products, Inc.
1671 Cherry Street
Youngstown, Ohio 44506

Mass Machine & Stamping, Inc.
85 Northeastern Boulevard
Nashua, New Hampshire 03060

W. H. Maze Company
Peru 9, Illinois 61354

McKinney Manufacturing Company
820 Davis Street
Scranton, Pennsylvania 18505

Medalist Leitzke
P. O. Box 305
Hustiford, Wisconsin 53034

Melard Manufacturing Corp.
153 Linden Street
Passaic, New Jersey 07055

Melnor Industries
Moonachie, New Jersey 07074

Montgomery Ward
619 West Chicago Avenue
Chicago, Illinois 60680

Multi Parts, Inc.
Hamilton, Illinois 62341

National Lock Hardware
Rockford, Illinois 61101

The New England Lock & Hardware Company
46 Chestnut Street
South Norwalk, Connecticut 06856

Nibco, Inc.
500 Simpson Avenue
Elkhart, Indiana 46514

Nixdorff Lloyd Chain Company
Division of Nixdorff-Klein
    Manufacturing Company
P.O. Box 14828
St. Louis, Missouri 63178

Norman Prince Associates, Inc.
840 Seneca Street
Lewiston, New York 14092

Northwestern Steel & Wire
  Company
121 Wallace Street
Sterling, Illinois 61081

Oreck Corp.
100 Plantation Road
New Orleans, Louisiana 70123

Parker Metal Corp.
85 Prescott Street
Worcester, Massachusetts 01605

S. Parker Hardware Manufacturing Corp.
27 Ludlow Street
New York, New York 10002

Parker Kalon Division
USM Corporation
Campbellsville, Kentucky 42718

Peerless Faucet Company
P. O. Box 31
Greensburg, Indiana 47240

Peerless Chain Company
P. O. Box 349
Winona, Minnesota 55987

Peerless Hardware Manufacturing Company
Chestnut Street, 2nd to 3rd Streets
Columbia, Pennsylvania 17512

Pemko Manufacturing Company
5755 Landregan Street
Emeryville, California 94608

Penn Dixie Steel Corp.
1111 South Main Street
Kokomo, Indiana 46901

Perfect Line Manufacturing Corp.
80 East Gates Avenue
Lindenhurst, New York 11757

Phifer Wire Products, Inc.
Tuscaloosa, Alabama 35401

Philstone Nail Corp.
57 Pine St.
P. O. Drawer G
Canton, Massachusetts 02021

Phoenix Specialty Manufacturing Company
971 Stewart Avenue
Garden City, New York 11530

Plumbcraft
24455 Aurora Road
Bedford Heights, Ohio 44146

P.T.I. Dolco
P. O. Box 61038
Los Angeles, California 90061

Quaker City Manufacturing Company
701 Chester Pike
Sharon Hill, Pennsylvania 19079

Qest Products, Inc.
1900 West Hively
P. O. Box 1746
Elkhart, Indiana 46514

R. E. C. Corp.
47 Cedar Street
P. O. Box 59
New Rochelle, New York 10801

Raco
P. O. Box 4002
South Bend, Indiana 46634

Raymond Merchandise
Barnes Group, Inc.
Corry, Pennsylvania 16407

Reed Cromex
23150 Commerce Park Road
Cleveland, Ohio 44122

Reese Enterprises, Inc.
P. O. Box A
Rosemount, Minnesota 55068

Rexnord, Inc.
P. O. Box 98
Paramus, New Jersey 07652

M. H. Rhodes, Inc.
99 Thompson Road
Avon, Connecticut 06001

Richards Wilcox
Aurora, Illinois 60507

Ridgid Tool Company
400 Clark St.
Elyria, Ohio 44035

Rixson Firemark, Inc.
9100 West Belmont Avenue
Franklin Park, Illinois 60131

Robin Hardware, Inc.
1150 Metropolitan Ave.
Brooklyn, New York 11237

Rockwell
Building Components Division
Morgantown, West Virginia 26505

Rodon Products Corp.
P. O. Box 279
Southampton, Pennsylvania 18966

Russell, Burdsall & Ward, Inc.
8100 Tyler Blvd.
Mentor, Ohio 44060

Safe Hardware Corp.
Berlin, Connecticut 06037

Samson Cordage Works
99 High Street
Boston, Massachusetts 02110

Sargent and Company
100 Sargent Drive
New Haven, Connecticut 06509

Schacht Rubber Manufacturing Company
P. O. Box 770
Huntington, Indiana 46750

The Schatz Manufacturing Company
Poughkeepsie, New York

Schlage Lock Company
P.O. Box 3324
San Francisco, California 94119

S & D Industries, Inc.
P. O. Box 3607
San Clemente, California 92672

Sears Roebuck Company
Sears Tower
Chicago, Illinois 60684

Selby Furniture Hardware Company
17 East 22nd Street
New York, N. Y. 10010

Select-A-Spring Corp.
192 Railroad Ave.
Jersey City, New Jersey 07302

Slaymaker Lock Company
115 South West End Avenue
Lancaster, Pennsylvania 17604

Snap Products Corp.
624 West Jackson Blvd.
Chicago, Illinois 60606

The Stanley Works
195 Lake Street
New Britain, Connecticut 06050

Sierra Electric
P. O. Box 85
Gardena, California 90247

Sterling Factories, Inc.
4000 West Ridge Road
P. O. Box 8427
Erie, Pennsylvania 16505

Sterling Alloy Casting Corp.
P. O. Box 580
Rock Falls, Illinois 61071

John Sterling Corp.
11600 Sterling Parkway
Richmond, Illinios 60071

Stic Klip Manufacturing Company
777 Regent Street
Cambridge, Massachusetts 02140

Superior Fastener Corp.
9536 West Foster Ave.
Chicago, Illinios 60656

Teco
5530 Wisconsin Avenue
Washington, D.C. 20015

Teledyne McKay
850 Grantley Road
P. O. Box 1509
York, Pennsylvania 17405

Thermwell Products Company
150 East 7th Street
Paterson, New Jersey 07524

3-M Company
3-M Center
St. Paul, Minnesota 55101

Thyrocan Controls Corp.
20 Commerce Drive
Telford, Pennsylvania 18969

Titan International Corp.
Morgantown, West Virginia 26505

Torch Products Company
654 Crofton, South East
Grand Rapids, Michigan 48507

Townsend/Richline
2515 Pilot Knob Road
P. O. Box 3518
St. Paul, Minnesota 55165

Triangle Pipe & Tube Company
P. O. Box 711
New Brunswick, New Jersey 08903

Triangle Pipe & Tube Company
Fittings Division
300 Delaware Street
Archibald, Pennsylvania 18403

Travco Plastics Company, Inc.
4718 Farragut Road
Brooklyn, New York 11203

Tridair Industries
3000 West Lomita Boulevard
Torrance, California 90505

Trine Manufacturing
1430 Ferris Place
Bronx, New York 10461

TRW
United Carr Supply Division
1 Nevada Street
Newton, Massachusetts 02160

The Turner & Seymour Manufacturing Company
Torrington, Connecticut 06790

USM Corp.
Shelton, Connecticut 06484

Underwriters' Laboratories
1285 Walt Whitman Road
Melville, New York 11746

United States Brass Corp.
Division of Hydrometals, Inc.
901 Tenth Street
Plano, Texas 75074

United States Gypsum
101 South Wacker Drive
Chicago, Illinois 60606

Vaco Products Company
510 North Dearborn Street
Chicago, Illinois 60610

Varlen Corp.
P. O. Drawer 70
East Alton, Illinois 62024

Waterbury Pressed Metal Division
407 Brookside Road
Waterbury, Connecticut 06720

Waxman Industries, Inc.
24455 Aurora Road
Bedford Heights, Ohio 44146

Weiser Company
4100 Ardmore Avenue
South Gate, California 90280

Wej-It Corp.
Atlast Industrial Park
500 Alter St.
Broomfield, Colorado 80020

R. D. Werner Company, Inc.
P. O. Box 580
Greenville, Pennsylvania 16125

Wheatland Tube Company
Independence Square
Public Ledger Building
Philadelphia, Pennsylvania 19106

Winzeler Stamping Company
Montpelier, Ohio 43543

Wiremold Company
West Hartford, Connecticut 06110

Witco Chemical Polymer Division
291 Fairfield Avenue
Fairfield, New Jersey 07006

G. F. Wright Steel and Wire
Worcester, Massachusetts 01603

Wrightsville Hardware Company
Wrightsville, Pennsylvania 17368

Wrightway Manufacturing Company
371 East 116th Street
Chicago, Illinois 60628

Yorkville Industries, Inc.
55 Motor Avenue
Farmingdale, New York 11735

Ziabicki Import Company
P. O. Box 994
Racine, Wisconsin 53405

INDEX

INDEX